# lonely planet

**POCKET**

# TORONTO

Isabella Noble

# Contents

## Plan Your Trip  4

| | |
|---|---|
| The Journey Begins Here | 4 |
| Our Picks | 6 |
| Perfect Days | 16 |
| Get Prepared | 20 |
| When to Go | 22 |
| Getting There | 24 |
| Getting Around | 25 |
| A Few Surprises | 28 |

Top: Black-and-white warbler, Tommy Thompson Park (p136)
Bottom: Fort York (p51)

POCKET **TORONTO**

## Explore Toronto — 31

Entertainment & Financial Districts — 33
Waterfront — 49
Old Town & Distillery District — 61
Downtown Core & the Village — 73
Chinatown, Kensington Market, Queen West & Little Italy — 87
Yorkville, the Annex & University of Toronto — 101
Trinity Bellwoods & the West End — 115
East Toronto — 129

## Toronto Toolkit — 147

Family Travel — 148
Accommodations — 149
Food, Drink & Nightlife — 150
LGBTIQ+ Travelers — 152
Health & Safe Travel — 153
Responsible Travel — 154
Accessible Travel — 156
Nuts & Bolts — 157

## ★ Top Experiences

CN Tower — 36
Hockey Hall of Fame — 38
Ripley's Aquarium of Canada — 39
Fort York — 51
Worth a Trip: Toronto Islands — 58
Distillery District — 63
St Lawrence Market — 64
Elgin & Winter Garden Theatre — 76
Art Gallery of Ontario — 90
Royal Ontario Museum — 104
High Park — 118
Evergreen Brick Works — 132
Worth a Trip: Niagara Falls — 142

FROM TOP LEFT: DENNIS W DONOHUE/SHUTTERSTOCK, ROLAND SHAINIDZE/SHUTTERSTOCK

Lonely Planet respectfully acknowledges that Canada is the traditional territory of more than 630 First Nations communities as well as Inuit and Métis communities. We offer gratitude to the Indigenous Peoples for their care for, and teachings about, this land.

# The Journey Begins Here

One of my earliest Toronto memories is catching the ferry to the beautiful Toronto Islands for views of what makes this easygoing city sparkle, from the deep-blue harbor to the soaring skyline. Recent years have seen Michelin stars, major museum revamps, reinvigorated green spaces and creative urban-art projects. Whenever I'm in town, my go-to neighborhood is the East End, where I love catching city views over coffee in Riverdale Park, bar-hopping along Queen East and cycling through Tommy Thompson Park.

**Isabella Noble**
@isabellamnoble
Isabella is a Spain-raised, British-Australian travel journalist who often spends time in Toronto and has written over 50 Lonely Planet guides.

**Riverdale Park (p135)**
NAIBANK/GETTY IMAGES

PLAN YOUR TRIP

Alo restaurant (p98)

**THE BEST**

# Food Experiences

Nowhere is Toronto's famous multiculturalism more thrilling than in its kitchens. Most neighborhoods have a scene or cuisine, but there's fabulous food from all over the world across the city.

Be dazzled by the culinary wonders and ancient farmers market of **St Lawrence Market**, one of Canada's great fresh-produce hubs. (p64)

---

Taste diverse flavors, from fresh tacos to Jamaican patties, on a guided tour of **Kensington Market**. (p94)

---

Hunt down Chinatown's most delicious dim sum and dumplings at **Rol San** (p97) or **Mother's Dumplings**. (p98)

Hop between stylish haunts like **Oddseoul**, **Union** and **Haifa Room** on food-loving Ossington Ave. (p124)

---

Discover Michelin-worthy fine dining with a tasting menu at **Alo** or **Quetzal**. (p98)

---

Dig into a world of cuisines in Little Italy, from Caribbean-Latin at **Conejo Negro** (p98) to perfect tapas at **Bar Raval**. (p97)

### THE BEST

# Architecture & History Experiences

Toronto continues to grow into the sky as sweeping skyscrapers go up, while historical jewels reveal its past stories.

Zip up the 553m-high **CN Tower** (pictured) on a spine-tingling ride blending exquisite urban views with a marvel of 1970s architecture. (p36)

Be immersed in industrial heritage at the **Distillery District**, a former distillery turned hub for design, arts and cuisine. (p63)

Step into the 19th century at **Fort York**, the well-preserved site of one of the city's most devastating battles. (p51)

Stroll the **Entertainment and Financial Districts** to glimpse sparkling skyscrapers, hidden heritage buildings and open-air art. (p40)

Marvel at the castle-inspired shape of hilltop **Casa Loma**, with its turrets and chandeliers, while soaking up superb city views. (p108)

Wander the historic colleges, green gardens and thought-provoking Philosopher's Walk (pictured) at the **University of Toronto** (p107).

FROM LEFT: VALESTOCK/SHUTTERSTOCK, SHAWN.CCF/SHUTTERSTOCK

### THE BEST

# Art & Museum Experiences

Welcome to some of Canada's finest galleries, whether it's natural sciences that capture your attention or contemporary art that makes your heart sing.

Take in creative treasures at the **Art Gallery of Ontario**, where Group of Seven masterpieces (among many others) are on show. (p90)

Discover some of Toronto's most engaging street art, starting with the urban wonders of **Graffiti Alley**. (p95)

Roam the halls of the **Royal Ontario Museum** (pictured), home to dinosaurs, Egyptian mummies and Indigenous ceremonial poles. (p104)

See what's on at the **Museum of Contemporary Art Toronto**, where cutting-edge exhibitions inspire thought and conversation. (p122)

Learn all about footwear past and present at the **Bata Shoe Museum**, an eye-opening collection inside a shoebox-shaped space. (p108)

Dip a toe into the intricate world of beautifully crafted ceramics at the **Gardiner Museum**. (p109)

Right: Bata Shoe Museum (p108)

FROM LEFT: COREY WISE/LONELY PLANET, EUGENIO FILICE/ALAMY, © 2025 BATA SHOE MUSEUM, TORONTO, CANADA (PHOTO: PHILIP CASTLETON)

## THE BEST

# Indigenous Toronto Experiences

Known as Tkaronto in Mohawk language, Toronto is built on the ancestral lands of various Indigenous communities. From arts to food, there are many ways to engage with their cultures.

Glimpse masterpieces of Indigenous art, such as those by Norval Morrisseau at the **Art Gallery of Ontario**. (p90)

Drop by the **Native Canadian Centre of Toronto** (pictured) for its Indigenous-owned craft shop and expert-guided walks. (p108)

Enjoy traditional cooking rooted in sustainable practices and local ingredients at the East End's **Tea-N-Bannock**. (p140)

Take a guided walk with **Heritage Toronto**, with tours that shine a spotlight on the city's Indigenous heritage and cultures. (p69)

Hear storytelling and music with an audioguide created by Indigenous communities at **Niagara Glen Nature Reserve** (pictured). (p145)

Toronto Islands (p58)

**THE BEST**

# Green Spaces Experiences

Toronto might be known for its bold urban skyline, but there are plenty of places to escape into the greenery and get active outdoors (even in winter).

Sail to the **Toronto Islands** for beaches, kayaking and walking in a cottage-country-like setting with spectacular views. (p58)

Get lost in undulating beauty, where trails weave into woods and birds gather around ponds at **High Park**. (p118)

Paddleboard, kayak or canoe along the Waterfront – try the Humber River mouth near **Sunnyside Beach**. (p54)

Soak up the seasons in beloved **Trinity Bellwoods Park**, known for its spring blooms and fall colors. (p122)

Cycle, run or walk the wilds of **Tommy Thompson Park**, keeping your eyes peeled for local birdlife. (p136)

Follow the lakefront boardwalk along **The Beaches**, before braving the blue waters for a refreshing swim. (p136)

## THE BEST

# Entertainment Experiences

There's always something happening on Toronto's creative and sporting stages. Outdoor concerts and free festivals land in summer, but even during the coldest months the city keeps things grooving.

See a movie at the glowing **TIFF Lightbox**, the main hub for Toronto's star-studded film festival. (p43)

---

Catch a top-class live-music performance at a landmark venue with decades of history, like **Horseshoe Tavern** (p96) or **Massey Hall** (pictured). (p82)

---

Marvel at the Bard's genius during an open-air Shakespeare performance in High Park, courtesy of **Canadian Stage**. (p69)

Cheer on the Blue Jays at the awe-inducing **Rogers Centre** (pictured) or take a behind-the-scenes peek on a guided tour. (p42)

---

Be wowed by the magical design of the century-old **Elgin & Winter Garden Theatre**, staging a wide range of performances. (p76)

---

Dive into Canadian hockey at the **Hockey Hall of Fame**, where you can even play (virtual) games with sporting legends. (p38)

THE BEST

# Nightlife Experiences

Toronto nightlife embraces it all, from gritty dive bars going back decades to chic rooftop lounges, hidden speakeasies and sultry wine bars. In warmer months, it's all about street-side patios.

Dance the night away at one of North America's most fabulous LGBTIQ+ districts, the **Village** (p80).

---

Hit the Entertainment District's **rooftop bars** for drinks with dreamy skyline views, perhaps at **Evangeline**. (p47)

---

Savor cocktail ingredients designed to surprise at creative lounges like **Mother Cocktail Bar**. (p126)

Bar-hop on Ossington Ave, the West End's favorite late-night spot, including longtime haunts like **Sweaty Betty's**. (p127)

---

Seek out acclaimed East Toronto breweries, such as Czech-leaning **Godspeed Brewery** (p140) and **Avling**, with its rooftop veg garden. (p139)

Evangeline (p47)

**THE BEST**

# Neighborhood Experiences

Beyond the Downtown epicenter lies a world of distinctive neighborhoods, each with its own personality and backstory. Spend time wandering the streets and soaking up the atmosphere.

Weave through the peaceful residential streets of **Cabbagetown** (pictured left), known for its impressive collection of Victorian homes. (p134)

Seek out flavors from Seoul and beyond in **Koreatown** (pictured right), a lively stretch of the city centered on Bloor St W. (p109)

Wind back the centuries in elegant **Yorkville**, where the ancient heart of the neighborhood still shows off historical homes. (p109)

Head west to relaxed **Roncesvalles**, with its wonderful murals and leafy streets on the fringes of High Park. (p122)

Make the well-worth-it journey to the **Junction**, a former manufacturing community with original-period buildings, now turned arts hub. (p123)

Get a taste of Ontario's cottage country on **Ward's Island**, where colorful wooden houses overlook Lake Ontario. (p58)

FROM LEFT: SPIROVIEW INC/SHUTTERSTOCK, KOSHIRO K/SHUTTERSTOCK

# Best for Kids

Admire creatures of the deep at **Ripley's Aquarium of Canada** (p39), from gliding sea turtles to leopard sharks swimming the waters.

---

Feel the thrill of zooming up the **CN Tower** (p36) by elevator, for views that wow visitors of all ages and daredevil activities like walking on glass.

---

Discover the wonders of the **Royal Ontario Museum** (p104), a favorite among little ones for its collections of dinosaur skeletons.

---

Take the kids to meet the aimals at **Riverdale Farm** (p136), then visit neighboring **Evergreen Brick Works** (p132) with its educational children's gardens.

---

Pop into the **Distillery District** (p63) for hot chocolate with a side of history, especially during cooler months when the Winter Village market is on.

# Best for Free

Learn about a major battle during the War of 1812 at **Fort York** (p51), a National Historic Site offering free guided tours.

---

Explore the sidestreets to find some of Toronto's liveliest art spread across the urban walls, starting with **Graffiti Alley** (p95).

---

Take advantage of regular free-entry hours at standout museums like the **Art Gallery of Ontario** (p90), or check out what's on at the free-access **Harbourfront Centre** (p54).

---

Climb the stairs to **Spadina Museum** (p110), where volunteers lead free, engaging guided walks of a beautiful 19th-century country estate.

---

Dig into eastern Toronto's industrial history at **Evergreen Brick Works** (p132), a restored 19th-century brick factory with bold art, free tours and a farmers market.

# Perfect Days

Spending time in Toronto is as much about taking in its bright lights and headliner sights as it is about wandering the laid-back neighborhoods, so it pays to combine a bit of everything.

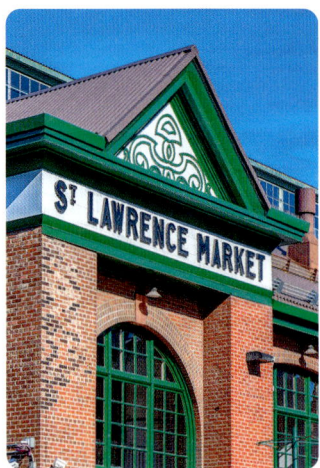

St Lawrence Market (p64)

### DAY ONE

## Only Have One Day?

**MORNING**

Head out early and make a beeline for the **CN Tower** (p36) to beat the queues for its 360-degree views. Afterward, pick between underwater wonders at **Ripley's Aquarium of Canada** (pictured; p39) or sporting history at the **Hockey Hall of Fame** (p38).

**AFTERNOON**

Wander into the Old Town along Front St and graze your way around historic **St Lawrence Market** (p64). Then spend the rest of the afternoon poking around the shops and creative studios in the **Distillery District** (p63).

**EVENING**

Enjoy dinner at **Pai** (p45) or **Gusto 101** (p46), then hit the theaters or catch a baseball game at the dazzling **Rogers Centre** (p42).

### DAY TWO
## A Weekend Trip

**MORNING**

Spend a few hours taking in the city's waterfront, ideally **cycling along Lake Ontario's shores** (p52) or checking out the creative **Harbourfront Centre** (p54).

**AFTERNOON**

Zip up Spadina Ave (either walking or on streetcar 510), hopefully stopping for lunch at **Cà Phê Rang** (p97) or a Chinatown classic like **Rol San** (p97) and peeking down **Graffiti Alley** (p95). Devote the afternoon to the **Art Gallery of Ontario** (AGO; p90) and vintage shops in Kensington Market (pictured) like **Hi** (p94) and **Courage My Love** (p94).

**EVENING**

Pick from some of the city's top tacos at Kensington's **Gus Tacos** (p97) or **Seven Lives** (p98). Or head west along College St for an evening bite at **Bar Raval** (p97) and cocktails at **Bar Pompette** (p96).

### DAY THREE
## A Short Break

**MORNING**

Begin day three at the **Royal Ontario Museum** (ROM; p104), one of Canada's greatest galleries. The adjacent **Philosopher's Walk** (p107) offers a breath of fresh air in the grounds of the University of Toronto.

**AFTERNOON**

After a smart lunch in Yorkville (perhaps **Trattoria Nervosa**; p111), pick between hopping south by subway to check out **Nathan Phillips Square** (pictured; p80) and Toronto's flying-saucer-like **City Hall** (p80), or heading north to explore **Casa Loma** (p108) up on the escarpment.

**EVENING**

Make your way over to the Village, Toronto's lively LGBTIQ+ hub, where beloved haunts include **O'Grady's on Church** (p80) and **Woody's** (p80).

# If You Have More Time

These extra recommendations work best mixed-and-matched with more classic Toronto itineraries. Spend time soaking up the greenery-filled **West End** (p115). A great option is brunch or coffee in Trinity Bellwoods – we love **Union** (p124) and **Found Coffee** (p126), followed by a stroll around lovely **High Park** (p118) or a creative immersion at the **Museum of Contemporary Art Toronto** (MOCA; p122).

---

Make a detour to **The Beaches** (p136) to stroll along the boardwalk, relax on **Kew Beach** (p136) and enjoy the local atmosphere.

Take a quick ride on the streetcar or subway to discover easygoing **East Toronto** (p129). Highlights include city views from **Riverdale Park** (p135) or the **Broadview Hotel rooftop** (p141), the sustainable marvels of **Evergreen Brick Works** (p132) and cycling in **Tommy Thompson Park** (p136).

---

Don't miss the haven-like **Toronto Islands** (p58), a green expanse just offshore, home to some of the city's finest beaches and water sports like paddleboarding and kayaking.

**Evergreen Brick Works (p132)**

## A City Day Trip

In a long, rewarding day trip, it's perfectly possible to visit spectacular **Niagara Falls** (pictured; p142) from Toronto, provided you start early. If you're keen to drive, hire a car for the day. Alternatively, take the GO train from Toronto's Union Station to reach Niagara Falls in 2½ hours. Once here, there are endless ways to enjoy the natural spectacle of the Niagara River thundering over the falls on the Canada–USA border. Find time, if possible, for a stroll in the gorge itself at the **White Water Walk** (p145) or the wilder **Niagara Glen Nature Reserve** (p145).

## On a Rainy Day

Toronto knows a thing or two about powering on during inclement weather. Start with **PATH** (pictured; p43), the Financial District's fascinating network of underground walkways and plazas. Major museums such as **ROM** (p104) or **AGO** (p90) can easily take up half a day, while other galleries worth visiting include **Bata Shoe Museum** (p108) and **MOCA** (p122). Then there's the performing-arts scene, whether you prefer ballet or opera in the Entertainment District, a cutting-edge play at the **Young Centre for the Performing Arts** (p69) or grooving to live music anywhere from Queen West's **Horseshoe Tavern** (p96) to the eastern **Opera House** (p141). Even staying indoors with a movie feels exciting at **TIFF Lightbox** (p43).

# Get Prepared

## BOOK AHEAD

**Three months before** Book tickets for high-profile events and concerts. If possible, reserve accommodations and fine-dining restaurants.

**One month before** Make dinner reservations at hot spots, especially for weekends. Book tours and sports tickets. Check dates for festivals, markets etc.

**One to two weeks before** Buy tickets for must-see sights and attractions. Reservations are still possible for local restaurants.

## Manners Matter

Torontonians are a fairly laid-back, friendly crowd and aren't easily offended; however, some rules of etiquette do apply.

'Please', 'thank you' and 'sorry' are highly valued words. Bumping into someone without apologizing or not thanking someone for holding the door is considered very disrespectful.

While Torontonians usually just tut when dismayed, jumping ahead in line can prompt full-on shouts.

## What to Wear in Toronto

Reflecting its diverse population, style here is all about a relaxed attitude and personal flair, so you'll see all manner of dress on the streets here. If you're visiting during cooler months, bring layers and hats – you can be freezing outdoors one moment, then peeling everything off once you step inside heated spaces. Upscale restaurants, theaters and bars require a smarter look. For beach days, keep it casual, with comfy footwear and swimsuits.

## Things to Know

**Tour timings** It pays to plan ahead if you're keen to join a guided tour, as many companies only operate from around June to September. Some tours are only offered on specific dates, too.

**Cafe culture** At many coffee shops around the city, it is polite to return your own used cups and plates; look for the dedicated (often labeled) trays.

**Winter etiquette** During cooler months, when someone is about to enter a building you're exiting, let them in first – they're a lot colder than you are.

**Shoes** Remove your shoes or boots and place them in the tray (plateau) provided in homes and B&Bs. Footwear brings in grit, mud and, in the winter, salt, which can damage carpets and wooden floors.

## TIPPING

Just like the rest of Canada, tipping is widespread in Toronto, especially for dining in restaurants and ordering drinks in bars, but also for other services such as taxis. Factor it in when considering prices.

- **18–25%** — **Restaurants**
- **$1–2 per drink** — **Bars** or 18%, depending on locale
- **10–15%** — **Taxis**
- **small change** — **Cafes & bakeries** or from 10%

## DAILY BUDGET

### Budget: Less than $100
- Dorm bed: from $45
- Self-catered supermarket meal: from $10
- Free sights and tours
- Subway/streetcar/bus fare: $3.35

### Midrange: $100–250
- Room in a B&B or midrange hotel: $180–260
- Meal at a good local restaurant: from $30 plus drinks
- Museum/sight admission: from $10
- Guided tour: from $25

### Top end: More than $250
- Double room in a four-star hotel: from $300
- Three-course meal at a top restaurant: from $70 plus drinks
- Food tour: from $100

**Currency**
Canadian dollar ($)

**Language**
English/French

**Time**
Eastern Time (GMT/UTC-5, -4 during daylight savings)

## MONEY-SAVING TIP

HAND-ROBOT/GETTY IMAGES

**Toronto City Pass** *(citypass.com/toronto)* offers a bundled rate for five attractions: the CN Tower and Ripley's Aquarium of Canada, plus three others from Casa Loma, Royal Ontario Museum, City Cruises and Toronto Zoo.

# When To Go

Toronto takes on a different feel with each season, from festive summer fun to moody fall colors. Winter is for hardy visitors who don't mind bundling up to explore.

From June to September, outdoor patios spring to life at bars and restaurants, a wave of festivals arrives and pop-up markets appear all over town. With temperatures climbing to the high 20s°C (low 80s°F), beaches get packed. Summer can be humid though, with some thunderstorms. Fall is a lovely, quieter time, with plenty of crisp sunny days and vibrant colors from late September to late October. Winter brings festive cheer, seasonal markets and ice-skating, but temps drop, winds pick up and many activities move indoors. Spring rolls around in April/May with gorgeous blossoms.

## Headline Celebrations

**May:** On the fourth weekend of the month, **Doors Open Toronto** unveils a wave of significant private and public buildings, with free visits and tours (book ahead); City Hall (p80) is often included.

**June:** One of the world's great LGBTIQ+ celebrations, **Pride Toronto** (p81) has parades, workshops, drag shows and other fun. Much of the action is centered on the Village.

**June:** Canada's **National Indigenous Peoples Day** is celebrated across town, with events including movie screenings, workshops and powwows. Fort York (p51) hosts the Indigenous Arts Festival.

**September:** The Entertainment District rolls out the red carpet for the **Toronto International Film Festival** (p43), when celebrities and celebrity-spotters pack into town.

## Toronto Weather

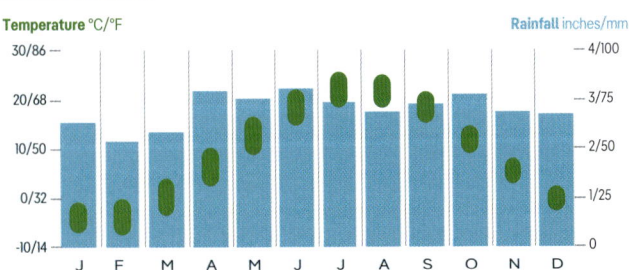

Distillery Winter Village (p63)

## Local Events

**June:** **Luminato Festival** brings some of the world's premier dancers, artists, writers, musicians, filmmakers and other creatives to Toronto, with many of the events held at the Harbourfront Centre (p54).

**July:** Ontario's largest performance festival has been going strong for 30 years and is still a star of the local calendar. Venues for the **Toronto Fringe Festival** include the Young Centre for the Performing Arts (p69).

**August/September:** First held in the late 19th century, the **Canadian National Exhibition** (or the Ex; p53) pulls in thousands of visitors with fair rides, agricultural shows, outdoors concerts and other events at historic Exhibition Place.

**November/December:** The chilly winter months are brightened up by the **Distillery Winter Village** (p63), which takes over the cobbled streets and 19th-century buildings of the Distillery District with festive craft stalls, sparkling lights and outdoor fun.

---

**ACCOMMODATIONS LOWDOWN**

Accommodations can be expensive all over the city, especially in summer, so it's essential to book ahead. There are often good deals in fall and winter. Big events, such as the Toronto International Film Festival, can send prices skyrocketing (check calendars in advance to sidestep them if required).

# Getting There

Many travelers arrive into busy Toronto Pearson International Airport, 25km northwest of Downtown. Other options include tiny Billy Bishop Toronto City Airport and Union Station, one of Canada's major transportation hubs.

## From the Airport to the City Center

### By Train or Bus
**UP Express** *(upexpress.com; $12.35, 12 & under free; every 15min, Union-bound 5:30am-1am, airport-bound 4:55am-1am, slightly reduced weekends)* is the fastest way Downtown from Pearson Airport, connecting with Union Station in 25 minutes. Tap in with a bank card or mobile payment. Express **buses** *(torontopearson.com)* link to Toronto's subway.

### By Taxi or Rideshare
A taxi to Downtown costs from $65. Rideshare apps like Uber sometimes offer lower rates. It can take from 30 minutes if the traffic is quiet to *much* longer at rush hour.

### From Billy Bishop Airport
A pedestrian tunnel links **Billy Bishop** *(billybishopairport.com)* on Toronto Islands with Bathurst St in six minutes. A free **ferry** *(every 15min, 5:15am-midnight)* travels 121m between the airport and Bathurst St – one of the world's shortest ferry rides (90 seconds). A frequent free shuttle **bus** links the tunnel and ferry stop with Union Station.

## Other Points of Entry

### Union Station
Toronto's main **train station** is housed in a beautiful Downtown building on Front St, served by **GO Transit** *(gotransit.com)* commuter trains, long-distance **VIA** trains *(viarail.ca)* traveling the Windsor–Montréal corridor and beyond, and even a few **Amtrak** trains *(amtrak.com)* heading to/from the USA. Arriving travelers have direct access to the subway at Union.

> **Union Station Bus Terminal**
>
> Both long-distance and local GO Transit buses run from **USBT** at 81 Bay St. **FlixBus** *(flixbus.ca)* and **Megabus** *(megabus.com)* serve Ontario and beyond.

# 🚈 Getting Around

The Toronto Transit Commission (TTC; *ttc.ca*) runs a wide-reaching network of streetcars and buses, as well as the city's three subway lines. Most destinations of interest to leisure visitors have public transportation options, with local taxis and rideshare services like Uber filling in the gaps. Toronto's notorious traffic is a beast, so it's best to avoid driving if possible.

### Subway & Train

The fastest way to travel around is on Downtown Toronto's two subway lines: U-shaped Line 1 (Yonge–University–Spadina) and east–west Line 2 (Bloor–Danforth). Services run every few minutes from around 5:30am to 1am or 1:30am. Stations have Designated Waiting Areas (DWAs) monitored by security cameras and are generally safe.

**GO Transit** (*gotransit.com*) commuter trains are also helpful for reaching a few places, such as Danforth Ave in East Toronto and Bloor GO Station near the Museum of Contemporary Art Toronto (p122).

### Streetcar & Bus

TTC streetcars offer frequent services across the city, with some routes operating 24 hours. Many of them run amid vehicle traffic, which means they can be slow during twice-daily rush hours. Streetcars pick up passengers at designated stops only; look for the small signs on the sidewalk or a dedicated streetcar stop. The main routes run

FROM LEFT: ACHPF/SHUTTERSTOCK, ESKYSTUDIO/SHUTTERSTOCK

---

**ESSENTIAL INFORMATION**

Check the TTC website for service updates, route planners and more.

east–west along College, Dundas, Queen and King Sts, as well as north–south along Bathurst St and Spadina Ave. To hop off, press the red 'stop' button or pull the yellow cord above the window once your stop is announced.

### Bicycle

Bike-rental agencies are found along the waterfront and charge about $15/40 per hour/day; try highly recommended **Wheel Excitement** *(wheelexcitement.ca)*.

For short rides, the citywide **Bike Share Toronto** scheme *(bikeshare toronto.com)* is a popular choice, offering both single-use rentals ($1 to unlock plus $0.12/minute) and day passes ($15 for unlimited 90-minute rides). There are docking stations all over the city, including the Toronto Islands.

### Boat

The main way to reach the oasis-like Toronto Islands is by catching a 15-minute ferry from **Jack Layton Ferry Terminal**, at the foot of Bay St on Queens Quay. From mid-April to mid-October, there are regular services to Ward's Island, Centre Island and Hanlan's Point. Schedules vary seasonally, but are roughly half-hourly throughout the season; in winter services run to Ward's Island only. On sunny days and weekends there can be long queues; arrive early or prebook tickets to save time *(toronto.ca)*. One-way tickets cost $9.11/4.29 per adult/child.

From spring to fall, a handful of water taxis also run to Ward's Island, Centre Island and Hanlan's Point from piers dotted along Queens Quay near the ferry terminal. **Tiki Taxi** *(tikitaxi.ca)*, **Pirate Taxi** *(piratetaxi.ca)* and **T Dot Water Taxi** *(tdotwatertaxi.ca)* all charge $13 for a one-way journey, with regular departures.

### Taxi & Rideshare

Taxis are easily hailed all over Downtown, often outside major hotels or Union Station. Metered fares start at $4.25, plus $1.75 per kilometer.

Rideshare services are readily available via Uber or Hopp.

### Car & Motorcycle

Parking in Toronto is expensive and traffic is horrendous, especially with the ongoing construction. If you must drive, remember to stop for streetcars – behind the rear doors when the streetcar is picking up or setting down passengers – and for pedestrians at crosswalks when the signals are flashing. Look out for cyclists in your blind spots.

City-operated Green P parking lots cost $1.50 to $6.75 per hour. If there's a special event on, expect a flat rate of $20 and upward for nearby parking lots.

# Public Transportation Essentials

### Fares & Tickets

The standard fare for a single journey on any TTC subway, streetcar or bus is adult/child $3.35/2.40 (children under 13 travel free). This includes a transfer which allows you to enter and exit the TTC as many times as you like within a two-hour period; it's particularly useful for journeys that involve changing between a streetcar and the subway.

### Digital & Contactless Payments

The easiest way to pay your fare on TTC, GO Transit or UP Express services is simply by tapping on with a contactless bank card or a digital wallet, either at the access gates or once on board.

It is also possible to pay by reloadable **PRESTO** card *(presto card.ca),* which is available as both a physical card (costing $4 at station machines) and in digital wallet format; PRESTO is mostly useful for local residents, but can also be helpful for visiting families with children, for example. The TTC also accepts exact (only) cash payments, though these don't include the two-hour transfer. As of 2025, TTC tickets, tokens and passes have been phased out.

---

**TRAVEL COSTS**

**Standard adult subway fare**
$3.35

**Bike/e-bike rental per half day**
$30/65

**One-way adult ferry ticket**
$9.11

---

**TAPPING OFF**

On streetcars, buses and the subway, there's no need to tap off at the end of your journey.

# A Few Surprises

From hidden-away landscapes to movie-starring family restaurants, Toronto is full of surprises – if you know where to look.

## Art on the Streets

Having kicked off in the 1980s, Toronto's street-art scene is a thrill, and walls all over the city burst with intricate murals. Many neighborhoods have dedicated projects to beautify public spaces with works by local artists, so keep your eyes peeled in areas like Queen West (p95), Little Portugal, Bloor St W, Riverside, Kensington Market and more. **StreetARToronto** *(street artoronto.ca)* publishes a handy digital map and guide to help you track down and identify some of the most exciting open-air pieces.

## Ravine Walks

Beyond the gleaming skyscrapers and urban energy, Toronto is a wonderful place to slip away into nature. It has one of the world's largest ancient ravine systems, carved thousands of years ago by receding glaciers that left behind rivers, valleys and meadows. Much of this now sits below the city, but it's still possible to enjoy some of these spaces, such as eastern Toronto's **Beltline Trail** (p136). Get a clearer picture of this special landscape at **Evergreen Brick Works** (p132), where a beautiful living work of art depicting the ravine system adorns the heritage building.

## Public Pools

When temperatures climb during summer, a favorite pastime is cooling off at one of Toronto's public swimming pools *(toronto. ca)*. The city runs a network of around 60 outdoor pools, open to all from roughly June to September (plus many year-round indoor options). Among the most popular is the lakefront pool at **Sunnyside Beach** (p56), as well as the one in

---

### OFFBEAT TORONTO

Pack in with regulars at classic dive bar **Sneaky Dee's** (p99), where the weekly trivia night is a crowded fixture.

In summer, spot the **Kensington Market Garden Car** (p93), billed as 'Toronto's smallest park'.

Impossible to miss on **Graffiti Alley** (p95), uber-5000's *Toronto Tribute* mural is full of in-the-know Toronto references.

Wander the Old Town and St Lawrence Market with actor-historian **Bruce Bell** (p68), a uniquely Toronto experience.

Patrician Grill (p70)

High Park (p118), where you'll be typically be joined by families, lane swimmers and sunseekers.

## On the Big Screen

You may have heard about Toronto's headline-making film industry, but often the city itself steals the show. Several old-school diners make regular silver-screen cameos; fans of *Confessions of a Teenage Drama Queen* might recognize Trinity Bellwood's 1930s **Lakeview Diner** (p125), while King St E's **Patrician Grill** (p70) has been hosting movie crews for three decades, including for Dan Brown's *The Lost Symbol*. Eastern Toronto bakery **Bonjour Brioche** (p139) and the bold **City Hall** (p80) both popped up in the HBO adaptation of Margaret Atwood's *The Handmaid's Tale*. And the entire city played a starring role in CBC/Netflix sitcom *Workin' Moms*, featuring the Victorian homes of **Cabbagetown** (p134).

## Literary World

There are thriving independent neighborhood bookstores here, many with lively calendars of literary events, from book-club discussions to launches of new titles and readings by resident and visiting authors. Places with a loyal following where you can join the fun include the West End's **Type Books** (p127) and **Flying Books** (p99) and eastern Toronto's **Queen Books** (p141).

# Explore Toronto

| | |
|---|---|
| **Entertainment & Financial Districts** | 33 |
| **Waterfront** | 49 |
| **Old Town & Distillery District** | 61 |
| **Downtown Core & the Village** | 73 |
| **Chinatown, Kensington Market, Queen West & Little Italy** | 87 |
| **Yorkville, the Annex & University of Toronto** | 101 |
| **Trinity Bellwoods & the West End** | 115 |
| **East Toronto** | 129 |

## Worth a Trip

| | |
|---|---|
| Toronto Islands | 58 |
| Niagara Falls | 142 |

## Toronto's Walking & Cycling Tours

| | |
|---|---|
| Art & Architecture | 40 |
| Cycle the Waterfront | 52 |
| Walk the Old Town | 66 |
| Downtown Core | 78 |
| Chinatown & Kensington Market | 92 |
| University of Toronto | 106 |
| Little Portugal | 120 |
| East Toronto Architecture & Green Spaces | 134 |

**Old City Hall (p79)**
FARUTXO/SHUTTERSTOCK

# Explore
# Entertainment & Financial Districts

These twin neighborhoods, centered on King, Adelaide and Richmond Sts, west of Yonge St, make up Toronto's beating, skyscraper-studded heart. Architecture marvels spanning several centuries catch the eye, business-centric streets buzz with life and beloved landmarks such as the CN Tower draw droves of visitors. The Entertainment District is the city's performing-arts epicenter, while the Financial District's banking history dates to the early 19th century, with high-rise towers emerging in waves throughout the 20th century. King West, the pocket around King St between Spadina Ave and Bathurst St, is one of Toronto's liveliest dining-and-drinking destinations.

## Getting Around

### 🚇 Subway & Train
Line 1 has plenty of stops in the neighborhood within easy reach of all the major attractions. Union Station (p41) is Toronto's main rail hub; UP Express train services run to/from Toronto Pearson Airport.

### 🚊 Streetcar
Numerous lines pass through the Entertainment and Financial Districts, including east–west routes like 501 and 504, and the north–south 510 along Spadina Ave.

### 🚶 On Foot
Broad sidewalks and interconnected squares, combined with the underground PATH network, make this an enjoyable area to explore by walking.

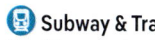

**Hockey Hall of Fame (p38)**
TODAMO/SHUTTERSTOCK

### THE BEST

**SPECTACULAR VIEWS**
CN Tower (p36)

**SPORTS CULTURE**
Hockey Hall of Fame (p38)

**URBAN ARCHITECTURE**
Art & Architecture Walking Tour (p40)

**FAMILY FUN**
Ripley's Aquarium of Canada (p39)

**ARTS SCENE**
TIFF Lightbox (p43)

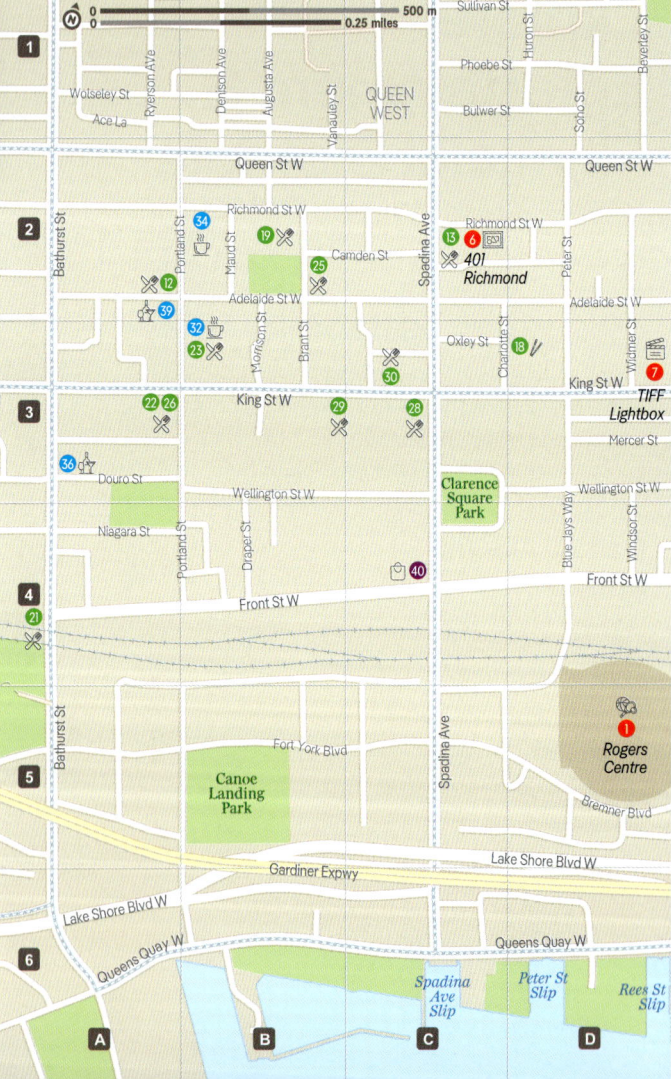

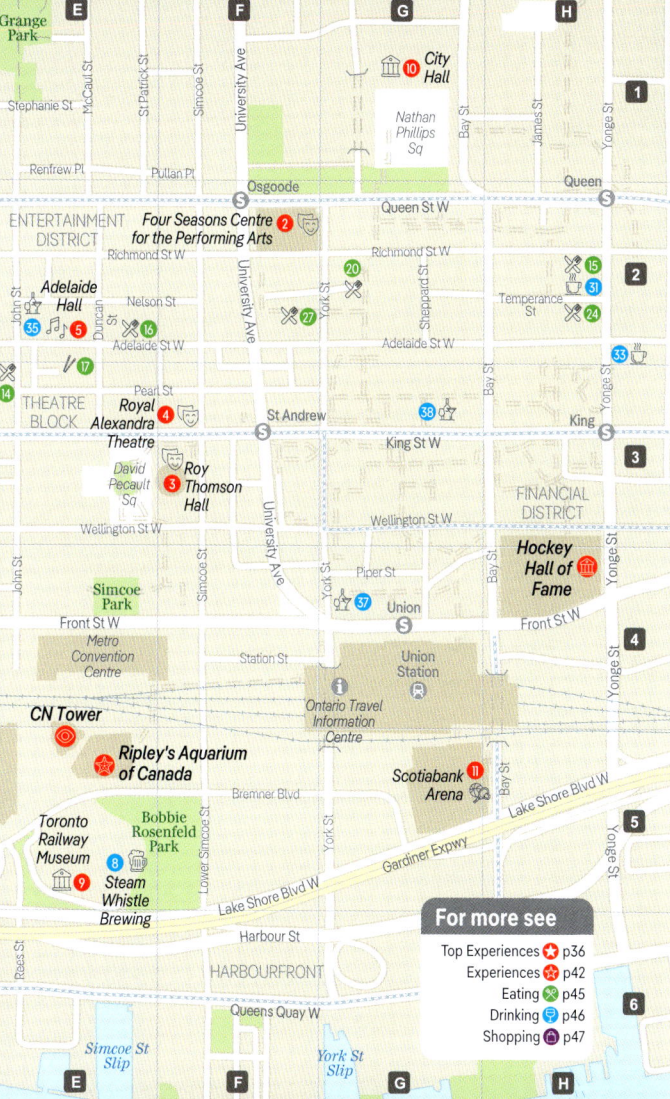

## ★ TOP EXPERIENCE

# CN Tower

Created during the 1970s building boom, the CN Tower is both a Toronto icon and an engineering marvel. Soaring 553m high near the lakefront, the concrete structure is worth the hype (and queues). Nothing prepares you for the spectacle of the 360-degree urban-jungle views or even the thrilling chance to hang off the exterior.

MAP P34 **E5**

**PLANNING TIP**
Beat the worst of the queues by booking timed tickets online in advance and arriving early. Check weather conditions ahead to ensure the best of the lofty views.

Scan for opening hours, reservations and more.

### An Architectural Triumph

Originally envisioned as part of a wider redevelopment of the area's railyards (which was eventually scrapped), the CN Tower was designed by Australian architect John Andrews in collaboration with local firm WZMH. It took 40 months to build with 1500 workers on board, finally opening in 1976. Until the arrival of Dubai's Burj Khalifa in the late 2000s, it was the world's tallest freestanding structure. Every night, the tower brightens up Toronto's skyline with a sparkling light show.

### Sky-High Views

In just 58 seconds, a glass-fronted elevator zips up to the **Main Observation Level** perched 346m above the city. As you wander around, floor-to-ceiling windows provide views of surrounding skyscrapers, the Toronto Islands and inky-blue Lake Ontario rippling into the distance. On a clear day, you might glimpse Niagara Falls across the lake. Sunset is a lovely time to be here, as the city lights begin to twinkle, but first thing is rewarding too, as you're more likely to enjoy some (relative) quiet.

From here, head down to the **Lower Observation Level**, where you can walk on a glass floor with views down to the ground 342m below, lean

ANNA BRZOZOWSKA/SHUTTERSTOCK

over windows thanks to the specially designed OverView space or step onto the outdoor terrace. Also here is an interactive art installation showcasing works by Canadian creatives.

### Extra Thrills

Those with nerves of steel can brave the 1.5m-wide, exterior **EdgeWalk**, which involves (safely) skirting the perimeter of the main pod while attached to a harness, with nothing between you and the city 116 stories below. Book well ahead. A wheelchair-accessible EdgeWalk experience is available on advance request. At 447m high, **The Top** observation level (an extra cost) is the highest of its kind in the western hemisphere – you can sometimes feel the tower swaying.

**QUICK BREAK**
**VUE Bistros** has pastries and coffee on the Main Observation Level. **360 Restaurant** serves upscale Canadian fare on a revolving platform. Or try Amsterdam Brewhouse (p57) on the waterfront.

★ **TOP EXPERIENCE**

# Hockey Hall of Fame

Within the 1880s Bank of Montreal building, the Hockey Hall of Fame is a Canadian institution. Even those unfamiliar with the rough, super-fast sport will be impressed by the world's largest collection of hockey memorabilia and interactive exhibits.

MAP P34 **H4**

**PLANNING TIP**
The entrance is on the basement level of the Brookfield Place shopping complex. Tickets are valid all day (so you can pop in and out) and best booked online.

Scan for opening hours, tickets and more.

### Collection & Activities

Spread across interconnected rooms and galleries, the hall charts the history of the game from its inception in the late 19th century all the way up to the present day's superstar players. The highly interactive space offers, for example, the chance to have a shootout against a virtual version of famous goaltenders like Carey Price.

Other highlights include walking through a replica of the Montréal Canadiens' dressing room, checking out the impressive collection of goalkeeping masks or trying your hand at hockey broadcasting in a model studio. And while there is a celebratory energy here, exhibits don't shy away from complex topics such as past discrimination and the sport's long path toward more inclusivity.

### Stanley Cup

The historical building's Great Hall provides a worthy backdrop for the gallery's beloved star piece, the Stanley Cup, which rests under a bright stained-glass dome and is awarded to each year's NHL (National Hockey League) playoff champions. You can also step into Lord Stanley's vault, where the original 1893 Stanley Cup (retired in the 1960s) sits on display with a collection of Stanley Cup championship rings.

⭐ TOP EXPERIENCE

# Ripley's Aquarium of Canada

One of Toronto's most-loved attractions, Ripley's Aquarium dazzles visitors of all ages with thousands of underwater species in creatively designed tanks. Sharks glide overhead, jellyfish loom out of the dark and fish flit through tropical waters.

MAP P34 **E5**

## Canadian & International Waters

The sprawling aquarium is usually busy, so it pays to aim for a few highlights, especially with little ones in tow. After admiring the enormous humpback-whale skeleton suspended above the atrium on the upper level, descend through the building's layers with a series of tanks devoted to Canadian water landscapes, such as freshwater lakes where sturgeon swim. Starfish, anemones, octopus and crabs mingle, before clouds of neon-colored tropical fish welcome you into the Rainbow Reef.

## Classic Highlights

For many, the aquarium's shining star is a glass-encased walk-through tunnel (with a slowly moving walkway) where sharks, rays and sea turtles float past as you make your way along. The nearby kids' crawl tube and the ray touch tanks are family favorites, too. Don't miss Planet Jellies, which evokes the eerie depths of the ocean through striking lighting for tanks containing hundreds of jellyfish. There's also a curious behind-the-scenes exhibit showcasing how the whole complex keeps things running and how saltwater is created on-site to mimic the oceans. The second Friday each month is jazz night.

**PLANNING TIP**
Sidestep the bulk of the aquarium's crowds by visiting outside the 11am to 2pm (4pm on weekends) rush. Allow a couple of hours to thoroughly explore.

Scan for full opening hours and to book ahead.

# WALKING TOUR

# Art & Architecture

The Entertainment and Financial Districts feature renowned architecture and attractions, as well as plenty of quiet corners. As the city continues to soar vertically, some skyscrapers now incorporate protected heritage buildings into their design, while open-air art installations bring a creative edge to the streets.

| START | END | LENGTH |
|---|---|---|
| Union Station | CN Tower | 2.2km; 45min |

### 1 Transportation Hub

Get started at Canada's largest railway terminal: **Union Station**. A Classical Revival beauty opened in 1927, it makes its mark with the entrance on Front St featuring 22 limestone columns. There's a great view of the nearby CN Tower from here. The highlight is the exquisite, light-filled Great Hall, with its provincial flags, cathedral-like ceiling and marble-clad flooring.

### 2 Castle Architecture

On the north side of Front St is the **Fairmont Royal York** hotel, built in the late 1920s by the Canadian Pacific Railway. It's one of Toronto's most memorable landmarks, thanks to its castle-inspired shape and green-tinged roof.

### 3 Rococo Jewel

A block east along Front St is the **Hockey Hall of Fame** (p38), housed in the elaborate rococo Bank of Montreal building. Head a block north on Yonge St, then turn left (west) on Wellington St. At Bay and Wellington Sts, you'll glimpse the Art Deco facade of the Toronto Stock Exchange (now an events venue).

### 4 Indigenous Art Collection

Continue west on Wellington St, passing the golden glass shape of Royal Bank Plaza. Pop into the free-entry **TD Gallery of Indigenous Art**, which hosts fascinating rotating exhibitions.

### 5 Urban Creatures

On the north side of Wellington St, zip through the small plaza of the Toronto Dominion Centre, a gleaming complex designed by Mies van der Rohe. Here you'll spot **The Pasture** – a group of bronze cows resting on the grass, by Canadian sculptor Joe Fafard. For a quick detour, Jaume Plensa's *Dreaming* (an 8.5m-tall marble-and-resin sculpture of a head) is a block north on Adelaide St.

### 6 Romanesque Revival

Emerging on King St, stroll 400m west to **St Andrew's Presbyterian Church**. Dating from the late 19th century, the stone revival building looks like a tower with parapets.

### 7 Arts Square

Hopping across Simcoe St into **David Pecaut Square** immerses you in the heart of the Entertainment District, offering benches, shade and pop-up events. Also here is the landmark Roy Thomson Hall (p42), with its gleaming glass facade shaped like a Jell-O mold.

### 8 Towering Icon

Wander south across Wellington St, then through Simcoe Park, where Anish Kapoor's bold *Mountain* sculpture awaits, evoking the beauty of the Rockies. From here, it's a 400m walk via a pedestrian bridge to the awe-inspiring **CN Tower** (p36).

## EXPERIENCES

### Catch a Blue Jays Game
SPORT

MAP: **1** P34 **D5**

As the only Major League Baseball team outside the USA, the Toronto Blue Jays are a source of enormous pride for any Torontonian. There is no better way to soak up the fervor than with the thrill of a live game at the spectacular 1989-opened **Rogers Centre** *(mlb.com),* the Jays' home base, during the April-to-October MLB season. Designed to accommodate up to around 50,000 people and with the world's first fully retractable dome roof, the stadium – one of Canada's largest – is an attraction in its own right. There's even a hotel built into it, with rooms overlooking the field. If the stars don't align for a game, hop on a tour *(adult/child from $40/25);* the standard one-hour itinerary includes field and dugouts access.

### Enjoy the Performing Arts
LIVE PERFORMANCE

MAP: **2** P34 **F2**

The excitement of attending a show among the leading lights of the Entertainment District is a classic Toronto experience. Overlooking Queen St and University Ave, the glossy, glass-fronted **Four Seasons Centre for the Performing Arts** is the go-to spot for top-tier performances by the respected National Ballet of Canada *(national.ballet.ca)* and Canadian Opera Company *(coc.ca),* which hosts a popular free-concerts series each summer. The classical theme continues at King St's **Roy Thomson Hall** (MAP: **3** P34 **F3**; *roythomsonhall.com),* home of the Toronto Symphony Orchestra *(tso.ca).* Lovers of musicals will want to check upcoming shows at the elegantly restored Beaux Arts **Royal Alexandra Theatre** (MAP: **4** P34 **F3**). For something more offbeat, pop into **Adelaide Hall** (MAP: **5** P34 **E2**), one of Toronto's finest small music venues.

### Get Arty at 401 Richmond
ARTS CENTER

MAP: **6** P34 **C2**

Stepping inside the red-brick walls of **401 Richmond** *(401richmond.com; free; closed Sun)* from busy Spadina Ave feels like entering an oasis of creative contemporary arts and urban greenery. Almost 150 galleries and studios led by a collective of local artists have set up shop inside a skilfully restored early-20th-century tin-factory building, which was once known for its fine lithography. It's worth looking for upcoming exhibitions and events, though simply strolling around and dipping into studios that catch your eye is fun too. The lobby houses a branch of popular **Dark Horse Espresso** and the excellent Spacing Store (p47; with original Toronto-themed design items), while the sprawling rooftop garden is a secret summer haven where herbs, flowers and vegetables grow.

### See a Movie at TIFF Lightbox
CINEMA

MAP: 7 P34 D3

A sparkling five-floor podium building on the corner of King and John Sts marks the headquarters and main venue for the Toronto International Film Festival, and its fabulous cinema complex. At any time of year, catching a movie at **TIFF Lightbox** *(tiff.net)* is the perfect way to get a taste of the city's famous screen scene. With five dramatically styled cinemas and a flowing glass-fronted atrium, the bold space spotlights independent films, world cinema, special talks and other events. Reserve ahead.

### Tour the Steam Whistle Brewery
BREWERY

MAP: 8 P34 E5

A crisp, refreshing Pilsner with bright-green bottling is the star at **Steam Whistle Brewing** *(steamwhistle.ca)*, a pioneering independent microbrewery going strong for 25 years and set inside the historic 1929 John St Roundhouse opposite the CN Tower. On the 30-minute guided tours *(adult/child $15/10)*, you'll learn all about the brand's backstory and sustainability initiatives while also scoping out the fine heritage building, which recalls how this area was once a major railway hub. Of course there's the chance to taste the locally popular brew along the way or at the on-site tap room with outdoor patio.

Also within the same complex is the small **Toronto Railway Museum** (MAP: 9 P34 E5; *torontorailwaymuseum.com; adult/child $14/5*), where you can climb on antique locomotives and dig into the city's rail history. Kids will love the summer mini-train.

### Go Underground at the PATH
STREET

Wondering how Toronto keeps things moving during the cold depths of winter or on stickily humid summer days? Then follow the Financial District crowd

---

 **TORONTO INTERNATIONAL FILM FESTIVAL**

Going strong since 1976, the Toronto International Film Festival *(tiff.net)* counts among the world's premier cinema celebrations and is a star-studded fixture on the city's calendar. Over 10 days in early September, King St is taken over by Hollywood legends, keen cinephiles and celebrity spotters. After calling Yorkville home for many years, the festival relocated to the Entertainment District and in 2010 landed its permanent base at the beautiful TIFF Lightbox. If you're visiting during TIFF, book everything well in advance (accommodations included), though last-minute screening tickets may be available.

### BEST GUIDED TOURS

**Heritage Toronto** *(heritagetoronto.org)* Historical, cultural and nature walks led by museum experts and historical-society members, plus self-guided routes.

**ROMWalks** *(rom.on.ca)* The Royal Ontario Museum (p104) runs excellent (free or affordable) walking tours with a historical focus, often in lesser-known districts.

**Culinary Adventure Co** *(culinaryadventureco.com)* Spirited food walks led by local experts, from Chinatown to Roncesvalles.

**Toronto Society of Architects** *(torontosocietyofarchitects.ca)* Volunteer-run walks with an architect's eye, including a Financial District towers itinerary.

**Toronto Bicycle Tours** *(torontobicycletours.com)* Cycle around the city with a switched-on team.

**Tour Guys** *(tourguys.ca)* Engaging pay-what-you like walking tours with an established operator.

---

down into the **PATH** *(toronto.ca/explore-enjoy/visitor-toronto/path-torontos-downtown-pedestrian-walkway)*, the city's beloved network of subterranean walkways. Extending across 30km and connecting 75 different buildings, the PATH runs all the way from near Queens Quay in the south to Dundas St W at the north end. It's a fun way to hop between sights and skyscrapers (or even sidestep the rush-hour traffic), and the whole place is packed with restaurants, shops, cafes and more. Whether you need a bottle of wine or a bunch of flowers, it's all here. The labyrinthine layout can make finding your way an adventure; a great place to dive in is Union Station (p41), perhaps weaving north toward **City Hall** (MAP: ⓾ P34 **G1**).

### Step into the Scotiabank Arena
SPORTS

MAP: ⓫ P34 **G5**

It's impossible to miss the colossal **Scotiabank Arena** *(scotiabankarena.com)* looming south of Union Station. As the hallowed home of the Toronto Maple Leafs (Stanley Cup winners 13 times), it's a must for fired-up hockey fans. The Toronto Raptors, Canada's only team in the National Basketball Association (NBA), are also based here. Leafs tickets are notoriously pricey and sell out fast, so plan accordingly (or try your luck for same-day tickets). For keen fans, the arena hosts expert-led behind-the-scenes tours *(adult/child $30/25),* with slots released three weeks ahead.

Just outside the stadium, 14 Toronto Maple Leaf legends are immortalized as larger-than-life statues in what's been dubbed Legend's Row.

# LISTINGS

# Best Places for...

$ Budget  $$ Midrange  $$$ Top End

See p34 for map of locations

## Eating

### Tacos & Cuban Bites

**Campechano** $$
⑫ A2

Fresh, homemade corn tortillas and ingredients from small producers are the key to the superb tacos here; fillings include roasted poblano peppers or spicy brisket. Also on College St. *campechano.ca; hours vary*

**Cubano Kings** $
⑬ C2

Miami-inspired, hole-in-the-wall cafe on Spadina started by a Havana-born chef. Enjoy smoky Cuban-style sandwiches with slow-roasted pork or Black Forest ham. *cubanokings.com; hours vary*

**La Carnita** $
⑭ E3

Happy-hour margaritas, daily specials and tip-top tacos (sweet potato, pork *al pastor*) pull in a lively crowd at this original location of a Toronto-founded Mexican fave. Several branches. *lacarnita.com; noon-11pm Sun-Wed, to midnight Thu-Sat*

### Canadian Cuisine

**Richmond Station** $$$
⑮ H2

*Top Chef Canada* winner Carl Heinrich is behind this smart, laid-back restaurant. Fresh-produce menus include charcuterie plates and leek-and-chickpea burgers with rosemary fries. *richmondstation.ca; 11:30am-2:30pm & 4:30-10pm Mon-Fri, 3:30-10pm Sat & Sun*

**Smoke's Poutinerie** $
⑯ E2

Cozy branch of a Canada-wide poutine specialist. A galaxy of options includes a fuss-free classic version and veg picks. *smokespoutinerie.com; 11am-11pm Sun-Thu, to 4am Fri & Sat*

### Thai Kitchens

**Pai** $$
⑰ E3

Stylish, buzzy northern-Thai spot with enormous bowls of *khao soi* (curry noodle soup) and other beautifully spiced dishes. Vegan options, too. Arrive early to beat the line. *paitoronto.com; hours vary*

**Khao San Road** $$
⑱ D3

Long-running Thai kitchen. Lively vibe and fiery menu of noodles, curries and other classics with your choice of spice. Attached is Bang Sue Bar. *khaosanroad.ca; hours vary*

### Food Halls & Markets

**Waterworks Food Hall** $$
⑲ B2

Top Toronto food-and-drink spots in a restored 1930s heritage building, such as cool wine bar Grape Witches and Kensington Market's Rasta Pasta. *waterworksfoodhall.com; 11am-10pm Sun-Mon, to midnight Thu-Sat*

**Chefs Hall** $$
⑳ G2

Upscale Financial District go-to, perfect for everything from morning espresso and artisanal cocktails to steaming ramen and fresh pasta. *chefshall.com; hours vary*

### Stackt Market 🍴🍴
 A4

Street-food stands, drinks options and rotating artist stalls fill this design-award-winning market near Fort York, built from reused shipping containers. *stacktmarket.com;* 9am-11pm Tue-Sun

### Italian Flavors

### Forno Cultura 🍴🍴
 A3

Pillowy focaccia sandwiches, irresistible pastries and other delights at an elegant King West bakery with communal seating. *fornocultura.com;* 7:30am-7pm Mon-Fri, 8am-7pm Sat & Sun

### Gusto 101 🍴🍴
 B3

An atmospherically renovated garage sets the tone for southern-Italian menus of delicious pastas, pizzas and salads, plus house wines. Fun summer patio. *gusto101.com; hours vary*

### Sud Forno 🍴🍴
 H2

Gorgeously redesigned heritage building with a chic all-day cafe (baked goods, espresso) and a smart upstairs *osteria* (housemade pasta, fresh pizzas). Part of the Terroni empire. *terroni.com;* 8am-9pm Mon-Fri, 9am-9:30pm Sat

### Creative Menus

### Alder 🍴🍴🍴
 B2

Trendy basement kitchen at the Ace Hotel Toronto. Mediterranean-leaning plates revolve around a wood-fired grill. Weekend brunch, too. *aldertoronto.com;* 5-10pm Sun-Thu, to 10:30pm Fri & Sat

### Lee 🍴🍴🍴
 A3

Chef Susur Lee's elegant and long-established flagship restaurant wows with its classic French and Southeast Asian flavors, starting with a signature 24-ingredient Singapore slaw. *leerestaurant.com;* 5-10pm Sun-Thu, to 11pm Fri & Sat

### Alobar 🍴🍴🍴
27 F2

Sleek restaurant-bar led by respected chef Patrick Kriss. Classic-inspired cocktails and light, fresh menus with wedge salads and steaks. *thealobar.com;* 11:30am-10pm Mon-Fri, 5-10pm Sat

### King West Hot Spots

### Miss Likklemore's 🍴🍴🍴
28 C3

Find a buzzing after-work energy and a long bar at this cool kitchen specializing in contemporary Caribbean cooking – cheddar biscuits, jerk chicken, peppery patties. *misslikklemores.com;* 5-10pm Tue-Sat, 10:30am-3pm & 5-10pm Sun

### Baro 🍴🍴🍴
29 B3

Latin American flavors fuel ambitious dishes like charred-jalapeño hummus and zesty yellowfish ceviche at a bustling multispace haunt with a year-round glassed-in rooftop. *barotoronto.com; hours vary*

### Beso by Patria 🍴🍴
 C3

Pair seasonal Spanish-style tapas (Manchego-cheese croquettes, spiced *patatas bravas*) with a sultry design-forward space for a classic King West evening. *besotoronto.com;* 5-10pm Sun-Wed, to 11pm Thu-Sat

## Drinking

### Coffee Spots

### Dineen Coffee Company
31 H2

A late-19th-century heritage building redesigned as a stylish cafe. Bright tilework, strong espresso and a sought-after corner patio. *dineencoffee.com;*

*7:30am-4pm Mon-Fri, 8:30am-4:30pm Sat & Sun*

### Jimmy's Coffee
 B3

This indie cafe's original Portland St outpost has a small patio, baked treats and Italian-style coffee made from house-roasted beans, plus a loyal local following. *jimmyscoffee.ca; 7am-6pm Mon-Fri, 8am-6pm Sat & Sun*

### Hale Coffee
 H2

Bringing specialty coffee to the Financial District, Hale is a switched-on Toronto roaster with several branches around town. *halecoffee.com; 7:30am-5pm Mon-Fri, 9am-4pm Sat & Sun*

### Fahrenheit Coffee
 B2

A standout independent coffee corner with a choice of seasonal brews from local roaster Omnia. Also on University Ave. *fahrenheitcoffee.com; 7am-4pm Mon-Fri*

## Views & Cocktails

### Evangeline
see 25 B2

Soak up the skyline over inventive artisanal cocktails and globe-trotting wines at the Ace Hotel's understated rooftop bar, with a terrace, lounge and great lobby bar. *evangelinetoronto.com; hours vary*

### Melrose on Adelaide
 E2

Perfect spot for a pre- or post-theater drink. A tempting menu of seasonal cocktails and Niagara wines, relaxed energy and a corner patio on John St. *melroseadelaide.com; 2pm-2am*

### Harriet's Rooftop
 A3

Creative cocktails (shishito margarita?) and Japanese-leaning bites at the stylish 16th-floor rooftop of King West's 1 Hotel. *1hotels.com; 5-11pm Wed, to midnight Thu, to 2am Fri & Sat*

### Library Bar
 G4

Take in Toronto history with your tipple at the swish, Art Deco–feel bar of the historic Fairmont Royal York, known for martinis with custom-made vodka or gin. *fairmont.com; noon-midnight*

## Local Haunts

### King Taps
 G3

Sprawling Financial District patio bar with 50-plus rotating craft beers, tasty margaritas and a good selection of alcohol-free drinks. Pub-style food includes truffle fries and fresh pizzas. Also on King West. *kingtaps.com; hours vary*

### Petty Cash
 A2

Popular King West 'social house' with killer cocktails, sports screens, daily happy hours, street-side patio, muraled walls and live music. *pettycashtoronto.com; 5pm-2am*

# Shopping

## Crafts & Fashion

### Spacing Store
see 6 C2

*Spacing* magazine's shop at 401 Richmond (p42) has original pieces spotlighting the city's diverse neighborhoods, from colorful prints to logo-scrawled sweatshirts. *spacingstore.ca; 11am-6pm Tue-Sat, noon-5pm Sun*

### Well
 C4

Seven architecture firms collaborated to create this glossy, sustainably focused mall and multi-use space on lower Spadina, with all the favorite fashion brands and a great food court. *thewelltoronto.ca; 11am-7pm*

# Explore
# Waterfront

Lake Ontario's shoreline is Toronto's great outdoor playground. Laced with traffic-free trails, lush parks and skyline views, this green lung is where Torontonians come to walk, run, cycle, rollerblade, kayak and more, and retains a local feel. Once home to railways, ships and industrial buildings, much of the Waterfront has been revived since the 1970s. Offshore is the beachy haven of the Toronto Islands (p58), while Fort York, one of the city's key historical sites, awaits just inland. During warmer months the whole place buzzes with outdoor patios, cultural events and pop-up markets; in quieter winter, there's ice skating and festive fun (though some businesses close). The Waterfront's eastward continuation is a treat too, especially around Tommy Thompson Park (p136).

## Getting Around

### Walking & Cycling
The Martin Goodman Trail weaves all along Toronto's Waterfront, making this an ideal area to explore on foot or by cycling through leafy green spaces. Convenient bicycle-hire companies include **Wheel Excitement** *(wheelexcitement.ca),* with rentals from $15.

### Public Transportation
Streetcars 509 and 510 run along Queens Quay W. Lines 503 and 504 along King St are also useful. The closest subway station is Union, 10 minutes' walk north of Queens Quay.

---

★

**THE BEST**

**OUTDOOR ACTIVITY**
Martin Goodman Trail (p55)

**HISTORY**
Fort York (p51)

**FUN ON THE WATER**
Kayaking & paddleboarding (p54)

**ART SCENE**
Harbourfront Centre (p54)

**GREEN SPACE**
Toronto Music Garden (p55)

---

Humber Bay Arch Bridge (p53)
BILL BROOKS/ALAMY

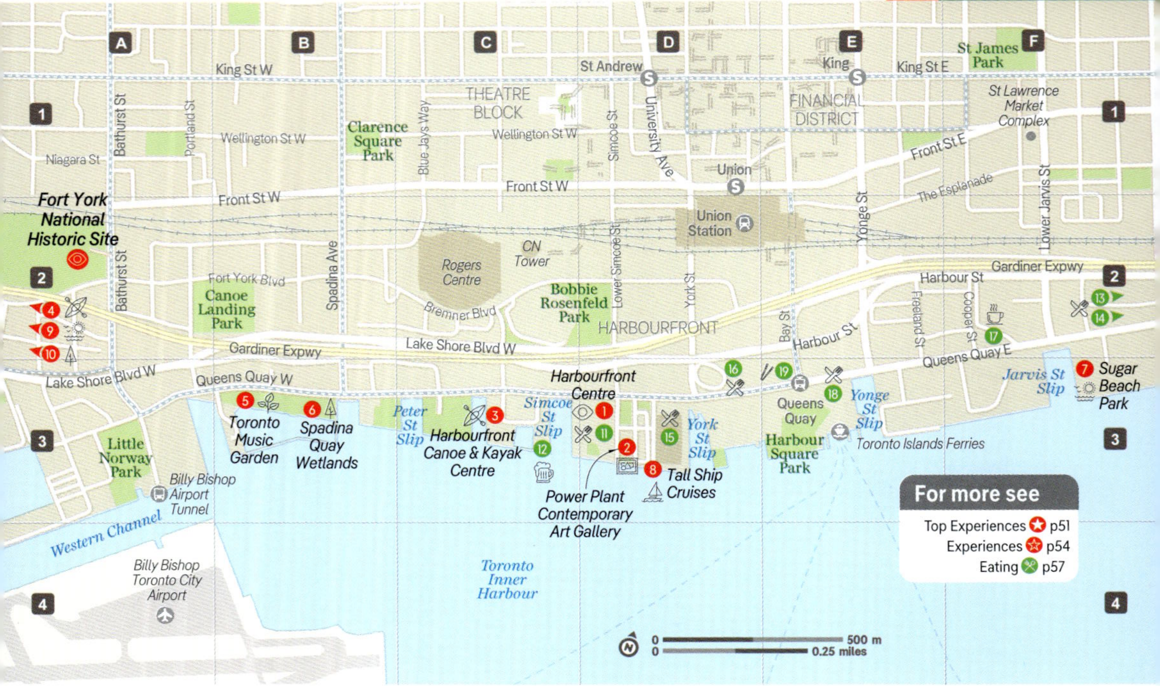

# WATERFRONT

## EXPLORE

### For more see
- Top Experiences p51
- Experiences p54
- Eating p57

**Map labels:**

- Fort York National Historic Site
- St James Park
- St Lawrence Market Complex
- Financial District
- Union Station
- Theatre Block
- CN Tower
- Rogers Centre
- Bobbie Rosenfeld Park
- Clarence Square Park
- Canoe Landing Park
- Toronto Music Garden
- Spadina Quay Wetlands
- Little Norway Park
- Billy Bishop Toronto City Airport
- Harbourfront Centre
- Harbourfront Canoe & Kayak Centre
- Power Plant Contemporary Art Gallery
- Tall Ship Cruises
- Harbour Square Park
- Sugar Beach Park
- Toronto Islands Ferries
- Toronto Inner Harbour
- Western Channel
- Airport Tunnel

**Slips:** Peter St Slip, Simcoe St Slip, York St Slip, Yonge St Slip, Jarvis St Slip

**Streets:** Niagara St, King St W, Bathurst St, Portland St, Front St W, Blue Jays Way, Wellington St W, Bremner Blvd, Lake Shore Blvd W, Spadina Ave, Queens Quay W, Fort York Blvd, Gardiner Expwy, University Ave, Simcoe St, Lower Simcoe St, York St, Bay St, Yonge St, Harbour St, Freeland St, Queens Quay E, Cooper St, Lower Jarvis St, Jarvis St, Lower Jarvis St, Front St E, King St E, The Esplanade, St Andrew, King, Union

Scale: 500 m / 0.25 miles

★ **TOP EXPERIENCE**

# Fort York National Historic Site

The sight of Fort York amid 17 grassy hectares, with the CN Tower and skyscrapers rising behind, is a curious snapshot of Toronto's identity today. Established by the British in 1793, the fort was rebuilt after being damaged in the War of 1812.

MAP P50 **A2**

### A Former Battleground
Originally built to defend the town of York (on what was then the waterfront), the fort was almost completely destroyed during the violent Battle of York in 1813, when US troops defeated a force of Ojibwe and British fighters. It was reconstructed soon after and remained in military use until the early 1930s.

### Exploring Fort York
Accessed from Fort York Blvd, the visitors center has a walk-through multimedia display evoking the 1813 events. You can wander through the site's scattered structures, which include basic 1815 soldiers barracks and an officers' mess from 1826, complete with liquor cabinet. A highlight is the 1813 Centre Blockhouse, Fort York's oldest remaining building, with exhibits focused on British military technology over the centuries and the Black contribution to the defence of Upper Canada.

### Indigenous Heritage
Each June as part of National Indigenous Peoples Day in Canada, Fort York is the setting for the **Na-Me-Res Pow Wow & Indigenous Arts Festival** *(nameres.org),* with a raft of events from culinary experiences and craft displays to dance, drumming and music.

**PLANNING TIP**
Free 45-minute guided tours run hourly and offer an excellent introduction to the site and the various identities at play in its embattled story. In summer there are live marching and musket demonstrations.

Scan for opening hours, tour details and more.

# CYCLING TOUR

# Cycle the Waterfront

A rewarding way to admire the beauty of the Waterfront is by weaving past its parks, gardens and beaches on two wheels. This easy route (also great for running or a long walk) takes in arguably the prettiest stretch of the lakefront, with much of it tracking along the locally loved Martin Goodman Trail (p55).

| START | END | LENGTH |
|---|---|---|
| Harbourfront Centre | Humber Bay Arch Bridge | 8.5km; 1hr (one way) |

### 1 Creative Hub

After picking up some wheels on Queens Quay W, check out the open-air art installations and revitalized industrial-era architecture at the fabulous **Harbourfront Centre** (p54), with its lakefront theater and winter-season ice-skating rink.

### 2 Urban Beach

Pick up the Martin Goodman Trail (parallel to Queens Quay W). Head 700m west to **HTO Park**, where Muskoka chairs sit under pastel-yellow umbrellas on a golden artificial beach. It was envisioned by Québec-born architect Claude Cormier, with willows and maples, and is great for spotting planes landing at tiny Billy Bishop Airport on the Toronto Islands.

### 3 Lyrical Gardens

Around 500m further on is the **Toronto Music Garden** (p55), designed to bring Bach's famed melodies into a physical space with astounding success.

### 4 Hidden Art

Another 500m west along the bike path is **Little Norway Park**. A pause here among the greenery allows a glimpse of an intricately carved ceremonial pole from the 1980s, *Dreamwork of the Whales,* which was created by a collective of British Columbia–based, Toronto-born artists.

### 5 Lakefront Park

Spin 1km onward past the 1930s **Coronation Park**, known for its gentle landscape of maple trees spreading around a grand oak and memorials for WWI and WWII (also a lively dog park).

### 6 Historical Site

On the north side of Lake Shore Blvd you'll glimpse the 1920s Princes' Gates arches of **Exhibition Place**, on a site that was once an important portage stop for Indigenous communities and later held both the French-built Fort Rouillé and the British Stanley Barracks. Now it's host to the three-week **Canadian National Exhibition** (CNE, or the Ex) every August/September, with fair rides, live music and other thrills.

### 7 Beach Culture

Zip 4km further west to eventually reach **Sunnyside Beach** (p56), popular for its calm swimming, water sports and public lake-view pool.

### 8 River Landmark

From Sunnyside, a 2km pedal through lakeside greenery leads to **Humber Bay Arch Bridge** at the mouth of the Humber River. Note the detailed geometric design, which pays homage to southern Ontario's Indigenous heritage. Pause to take in skyline views, then simply retrace your route.

## EXPERIENCES

### Admire Art & Crafts at the Harbourfront Centre  ARTS CENTER

MAP: ① P50 **D3**

Spread across 4 acres of lakefront land, the **Harbourfront Centre** *(harbourfrontcentre.com; free)* is a nonprofit art-world powerhouse with a thrilling year-round calendar of exhibitions, events and performances. It's best to check what's on in advance and plan around attending a particular event or exhibit, though you can also simply pop in at some spaces such as the Craft & Design Studios (in the main building), where the artists-in-residence work in public view. There are also event craft workshops you can join, such as textile art, glassblowing or jewelry-making.

### Catch an Exhibition at Power Plant Contemporary Art Gallery  GALLERY

MAP: ② P50 **D3**

For art lovers, a major highlight along the waterfront is the **Power Plant Contemporary Art Gallery** *(thepowerplant.org; free; closed Mon/Tue)*. This thoughtfully restored 1920s warehouse with a soaring red-brick smokestack is the setting for one of Toronto's premier contemporary-art spaces, with changing exhibits from Canadian and international artists. No matter when you visit, shows at this nonprofit venue are typically designed to spark conversations, break new ground and engage with current issues. It also hosts creative art-centric workshops for kids (book ahead).

### Go For a Paddle on Lake Ontario  WATER SPORTS

MAP: ③ P50 **C3**

Ask around locally and you're bound to be told that the best views of the city are from out on the water, where you can drink in the full heights of sky-reaching architecture set against Lake Ontario's deep-blue hues. Conveniently based near HTO Park, **Harbourfront Canoe & Kayak Centre** *(paddletoronto.com)* has kayak, canoe and paddleboard rentals *(from $50)*, with a map of recommended routes for anyone keen to explore the Toronto Islands. There are also expert-guided tandem-kayak tours *($85)*, for which no prior experience is required.

Along the western waterfront (near High Park), Indigenous-owned **Oceah Oceah SUP & Yoga** (MAP: ④ P50 **A2**; *oceahoceah.com*) offers the chance to paddle near the mouth of the Humber River or in the calm waters around Sunnyside Beach, with kayak and paddleboard rentals *(from $30)*, a variety of guided tours and even SUP yoga. The season typically runs from June to September and advance reservations are highly recommended for all activities.

### Relax in Waterfront Gardens

PARK

MAP: ⑤ P50 B3

Urban landscaping meets musical beauty at the **Toronto Music Garden** (toronto.ca), a free-access space stretching along the lakefront near the south end of Spadina Ave. Created in collaboration with renowned cellist Yo-Yo Ma, its flowing shapes, meandering trails and conifer groves were designed as a physical celebration of Bach's *First Suite for Unaccompanied Cello*. During summer, it's a magical spot to catch a free concert (check schedules ahead). At other times, taking a pause among the willow trees and wildflowers while gazing across to the Toronto Islands (see p58) is a tonic, and even during colder months the gardens provide a refreshing retreat amid the buzzing cityscape.

Just east of the Music Garden, a former parking lot was beautifully revived in the 1990s as the **Spadina Quay Wetlands** (MAP: ⑥ P50 B3), now a 2800-sq-meter oasis of indigenous plants where birds, butterflies and other creatures (even the odd beaver) gather. You're also bound to spot the undulating wavedeck right next to it, built to accommodate a regenerative fish habitat beneath.

### Soak Up the Views from Sugar Beach

BEACH, PARK

MAP: ⑦ P50 F3

An expanse of baby-pink umbrellas fringed by weeping willows and maple trees marks the pale sands of **Sugar Beach Park**, near Sherbourne Common just off Queens Quay E. It isn't exactly an urban beach (swimming isn't permitted), but nonetheless makes a refreshingly relaxed spot for kicking back on a lakefront deckchair, with the Toronto Islands just across the water. There's even a maple-leaf splash pad for cooling off, which younger visitors tend to love.

Designed by Canadian architect Claude Cormier, Sugar Beach kicked off the renewal of green spaces in this waterfront area and takes its name from the adjoining 1950s Redpath Sugar Refinery, where you might still spot ships docking. It's also perfect for a picnic, perhaps after buying a few snacks at Old Toronto's wonderful St Lawrence Market Complex (p64), just a 10-minute walk away.

---

 **MARTIN GOODMAN TRAIL**

The 22km-long Martin Goodman Trail (MGT) travels all the way along Toronto's shoreline from Humber Bay Arch Bridge in the west to the Rouge River in the east, providing a flat, vehicle-free path for walking, running and cycling. It's easy to pick up at any point and is a great place to enjoy Toronto like a local. The trail is also part of the still-in-development 3600km Great Lakes Waterfront Trail.

### Cruise the Lake                    TOUR
MAP: **8** P50 **D3**

If a low-key boating excursion around Toronto's harbor appeals, head down to Queens Quay Terminal (a converted 20th-century warehouse on the waterfront), where a crop of cruise operators gathers.

Well-established **Tall Ship Cruises** *(tallshipcruisestoronto.com)* offers daytime and sunset spins, including aboard the popular 1930 German trading schooner *Kajama (adult/child $38/28)*. **City Cruises** *(cityexperiences.com)* has its own array of excursions, such as a one-hour boat trip *(from $33)* with live narration as you trundle past icons like the CN Tower (p36).

### Have a Swim at Sunnyside         BEACH, POOL
MAP: **9** P50 **A2**

On summer days, **Sunnyside Beach** on the western waterfront is a hive of activity, with kayaks, volleyball, a boardwalk and people having a dip in the lake. Located just south of **High Park** (MAP: **10** P50 **A2**), this is a beloved spot to join a local crowd for some beach time – a breakwater just offshore makes for calmer waters.

Fronting the sand is **Sunnyside Bathing Pavilion**, a 1922 Beaux Arts building designed by architect Alfred Chapman. It was created with space for 7700 bathing lockers at a time when Sunnyside was one of the city's premier summer meeting points for swimming in the lake or an enormous heated pool known as the Tank. Don't miss the main north-facing facade, with its Classical columns and intricate tilework. The building now houses a waterfront cafe.

There's also seasonal swimming to enjoy at the attached **Sunnyside Gus Ryder Outdoor Pool** *(toronto.ca)*, one of several city-operated swimming pools with free entry and accessible services.

## LISTINGS

# Best Places for...

$ Budget  $$ Midrange  $$$ Top End

**See p50** for map of locations

## Eating & Drinking

### Waterfront Views

**Boxcar Social** $$
**11** D3

Overlooking Lake Ontario, stylish Boxcar is at its best on the lively patio, where specialty coffee, Ontario wines, breakfast sandwiches and mezze bowls are served. *boxcarsocial.ca; hours vary*

**Amsterdam Brewhouse** $$
**12** C3

Popular brewer with its own craft lager, wood-oven pizzas, smoky burgers, power bowls and waterfront seating. *amsterdambeer.com; 11am-11pm Sun-Thu, to 1am Fri & Sat*

**Simona** $$
**13** F2

Cool all-day spot with tempting contemporary Italian dishes like fresh pastas and burrata salads, just steps from Sugar Beach. *fabrestaurants.ca; hours vary*

### BBQ & Quick Bites

**Cherry St Bar-B-Que** $$
**14** F2

Try Southern BBQ classics like its signature Texas-style brisket at this converted early-20th-century building in the redeveloping Port Lands area. *cherrystbbq.com; 11:30am-10pm Mon-Fri, 11am-10pm Sat & Sun*

**Queens Quay Terminal** $
**15** D3

A 1920s warehouse transformed into a relaxed food court with waterfront terraces and a handy Farm Boy supermarket with take-out counters (perfect for picnics). *queensquayterminal.ca; hours vary*

**Impact Kitchen** $$
**16** D3

Join locals at alfresco tables overlooking Love Park for fresh bites like zesty Mexico-inspired salads and colorful fruit bowls at a health-focused Toronto chain. *impactkitchen.com; hours vary*

### Coffee Time

**Dark Horse Espresso** $
**17** F2

East End roaster branch pouring seasonal brews and serving delicious fresh cookies, croissants, muffins, breakfast sandwiches and other treats. *darkhorseespresso.com; 7am-5pm Mon-Fri, 8am-4pm Sat & Sun*

### Fine Dining

**Don Alfonso 1890** $$$
**18** E3

Sparkling views dazzle at this 38th-floor Michelin-star address, known for elevated, farm-to-table Italian menus featuring homegrown ingredients. *donalfonsotoronto.com; 5-11pm Sun & Tue-Thu, to midnight Fri & Sat*

**Miku Toronto** $$$
**19** E3

Mural-walled Japanese kitchen from the well-known Aburi Group. Delectable flame-seared sushi, tasting menus and à la carte options. *mikutoronto.com; noon-9pm Mon & Sun, to 10pm Fri & Sat, 11:30am-9pm Tue-Thu*

★ WORTH A TRIP

# Toronto Islands

Just a 10-minute ferry ride from downtown Toronto's bustle, this oasis of 15 interconnected islands offers a taste of wild, green Canada. With willow-shaded trails, cottage-like houses and dazzling skyline views, the traffic-free Toronto Islands (or Toronto Island) are a delight to explore, whether that's by walking and cycling or paddling the waterways.

**GETTING THERE**
Frequent ferries *(adult/child $9/4)* run from **Jack Layton Ferry Terminal** to Ward's Island year-round and to Centre Island and Hanlan's Point mid-April to mid-October. Schedules are seasonal. Private water taxis are an alternative.

### A Green Haven

Wrapped in a lush canopy, the islands have been a gathering place for Indigenous Peoples for thousands of years. Over 200 species of birds have been recorded here, while flora includes cottonwoods, ash, willows and cherry trees. The best ways to get around are on foot and by bike. On warm weekends, head over early to beat the crowds. The islands extend 5km from the east end of **Ward's Island** (the small residential pocket) to Hanlan's Point Beach in the west, all linked by flat, mostly paved paths. A scenic lakefront boardwalk connects Ward's with (busier) **Centre Island**, which has a small amusement park, picnic benches, food stalls and the 1809 **Gibraltar Point Lighthouse** (pictured). Toronto's bike-share scheme has docks at each ferry stop. You can also rent bikes at **Toronto Island Bicycle Rental** *(torontoislandbicyclerental.com; from $10)* on Centre Island, or at a mainland outlet such as **Wheel Excitement** (p26).

### Beaches & Views

With a gentle curve of soft golden sand fringed by greenery, relaxed **Ward's Island Beach** is one of Toronto's loveliest corners, perfect for swimming. Nearby **Algonquin Island**, linked to

Scan for islands and ferry info and more.

SELECTOR JONATHON/SHUTTERSTOCK

Ward's by bridge, has fine skyline views. The south side of Centre Island also has a calm sandy **beach** protected by a breakwater, popular with families. Bordered by low dunes, clothing-optional **Hanlan's Point Beach** stretches 2km along the western edge of the islands. It's the city's oldest surviving LGBTIQ+ space and has a lively scene (you can't miss the 600m-long rainbow walk).

## Adventures on the Water

One of the great joys here is gliding along the meandering waterways, where you might spot herons and swallows. **Toronto Island SUP** (*torontoislandsup.com; Jun-Sep; from $30*) rents kayaks and paddleboards beside Algonquin Island's bridge; book ahead. Its excellent guided-paddle experiences include a sunset route taking in the city lights.

**TAKE A BREAK**
Savor a flat white and fresh scone at **Runaway Cafe** (*instagram.com/ runawaycafeto*), a baby-pink coffee truck on Ward's, or lunch next door on the tree-shaded terrace at **Riviera** (*islandriviera resort.com*).

**See p70** for eating, drinking and shopping listings

# Explore
# Old Town & Distillery District

Red-brick industrial-era buildings, landscaped parks and cobbled streets draw people to the oldest part of modern-day Toronto. The Old Town sits where the former town of York was founded in 1793, and has a rich Indigenous history going back millennia. After booming with industry, then being regenerated in the late 20th century, today it's a lively neighborhood with galleries, shops, performing-arts venues and culinary riches. Many early structures were lost in the Great Fire of Toronto of 1849, so much of what remains dates from the 1850s onward. The Old Town's Distillery District is one of the area's top sights, while just north of it, Corktown is a residential neighborhood with restaurants, bars and Victorian homes.

## Getting Around

 **Walking**
This is a compact, pedestrian-friendly area ideal for exploring on foot and with a crop of leafy green parks to weave through.

 **Streetcar**
Frequent streetcars along King St E (503, 504) make various stops near both the St Lawrence Market and Distillery District. The 504A streetcar serves the Distillery District.

 **Subway**
The most convenient stops are King and Union, both on Line 1, with services every few minutes.

Distillery District (p63)
BOBNOAH/SHUTTERSTOCK

### THE BEST

**ART & DESIGN**
Distillery District (p63)

**MARKET MEALS**
St Lawrence Market (p64)

**URBAN LANDMARK**
Flatiron Building (p67)

**LIVELY SQUARE**
Berczy Park (p68)

**THEATER SCENE**
Young Centre for the Performing Arts (p69)

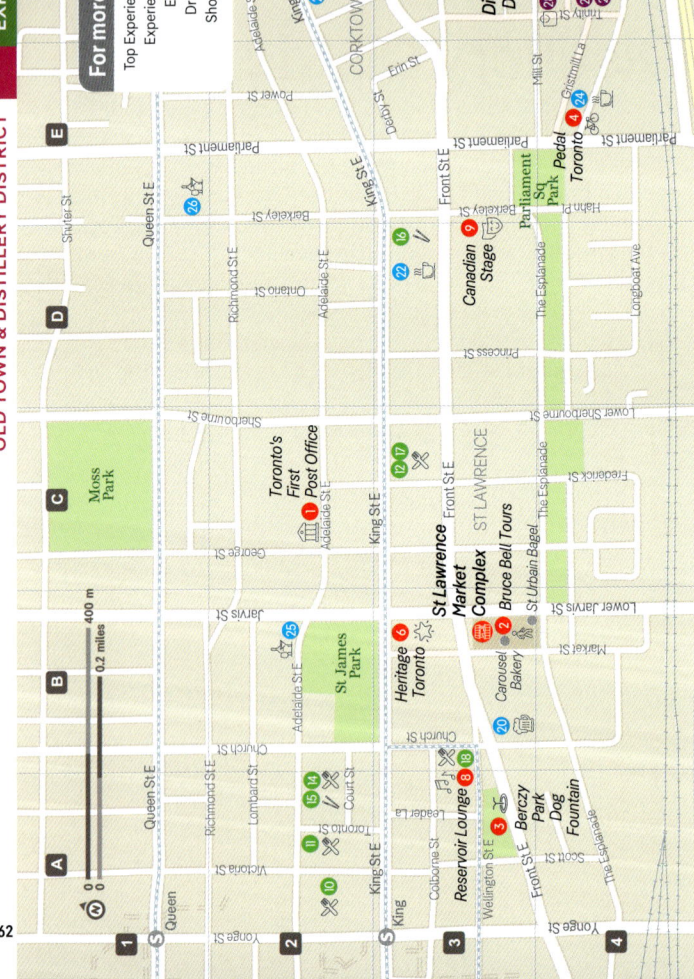

★ **TOP EXPERIENCE**

# Distillery District

The Distillery District is a visual feast of 19th-century red-brick warehouses and cobbled streets. Victorian industrial buildings have been beautifully restored as galleries, boutiques, bars and restaurants, while events range from jazz to Christmas markets.

MAP P62 **F4**

### Historic District
A National Historic Site with more than 30 Victorian buildings, the Distillery District was born in 1832 as a mill, before growing into the Gooderham & Worts Distillery, which produced mostly whiskey up to 1990. Many buildings are open to visitors, with industrial artifact displays and insightful panels about the city's largest spirit maker. The 1860 Stone Distillery is the oldest remaining building, hosting the Québec-focused Thompson Landry Gallery.

### Art & Design
Open-air art installations are sprinkled around the district. Standouts include Michael Christian's giant alien-like spider sculpture and Mathew Rosenblatt's steel peace symbol and red heart, all on Gristmill La. Arta Gallery, Beauchamp Art Gallery and Dish (attached to a Craft Ontario boutique; p127) offer exciting exhibitions.

### Winter Market
From mid-November to early January, the area morphs into the **Distillery Winter Village** *(the distillerywintervillage.com)* – a sparkling festive market with craft stalls, cabin-like counters serving hot chocolate and a Dior-sponsored Christmas tree. Some days require prebooked tickets.

**PLANNING TIP**
The Distillery District is at its liveliest on weekends, but also its busiest. For a more relaxed experience, drop by on a weekday. There are often evening events, too.

Scan for opening hours, events and businesses.

★ **TOP EXPERIENCE**

# St Lawrence Market

A market has been held in this area for around 200 years. Today the historic St Lawrence Market Complex continues to thrive as a beloved food destination, with 120 vendors stocking everything from cheeses to honey to fresh pasta, not to mention a locally popular Saturday farmers market.

MAP P62 **B3**

**PLANNING TIP**
The market is always lively, though weekdays can be less packed (note that it's closed on Monday). Plan to be here around a mealtime and allow at least an hour to enjoy.

Scan for opening hours, stall directory and more.

### A Tale of Many Buildings

The main event is **St Lawrence Market South**. Housed in a beautiful red-brick structure from 1902, it was built around the remains of Toronto's first City Hall (which stood here from 1845–99) and holds two floors of food stalls, delis and counters. At the north end, you can make out the shape of the former City Hall's council chamber, now home to the intriguing **Market Gallery** *(toronto. ca; Wed-Sun),* a small museum displaying photos, paintings and other relics from the market's past.

Across Front St, **St Lawrence Market North** relaunched in 2025 following a decade-long, multi-million-dollar revamp led by Rogers Stirk Harbour + Partners and Adamson Associates Architects (Rogers also designed Paris' Pompidou Centre). It's a boldly contemporary, five-floor creation with orange metal fins and a sweeping glass-walled atrium. At the time of writing, the building was only open during the Saturday farmers market.

### Global Flavors

From pillowy fresh Montréal-style bagels and Ontario-made cheeses to Italian olive oils and South American–style *arepas* (filled corn flatbreads), the

KIEV.VICTOR/SHUTTERSTOCK

market's two floors are a culinary treat, perfect for picnic items or products to take home. We highly recommend grabbing a bite from one of the stalls to enjoy at the bench tables dotted around the terrace – it might be your favorite Toronto meal.

## Weekend Markets

A feast of fresh regional produce, flowers and artisanal food awaits at the buzzing **St Lawrence Farmers Market**, which pulls in food lovers every Saturday from 5am in the gleaming north building. Head over as early as possible to bag the finest ingredients and best photo ops (and beat the crowds). Also worth catching is the stylish, all-day **Sunday Variety Market** *(sundayvariety.com)*, with vintage stores, antiques dealers and a DJ booth.

**QUICK BREAK**
Try Toronto's classic peameal-bacon sandwich in its **Carousel Bakery** birthplace or grab a cream-cheese bagel at **St Urbain Bagel** *(sturbainbagel bakery.godaddy sites.com)*.

# 🚶 WALKING TOUR

# Walk the Old Town

Branching off busy Front St, which once marked Lake Ontario's shoreline, this stroll immerses you in Old Town Toronto's charms. Weave past elegant Victorian buildings, green spaces, industrial-era landmarks and one of Canada's most spectacular produce markets while skyscrapers loom in the distance.

| START | END | LENGTH |
|---|---|---|
| Flatiron Building | Distillery District | 2km; 1hr |

## 1 Historical Treasure

Set against a dazzling backdrop of skyscrapers, the five-story **Flatiron Building** (or Gooderham Building) was created in 1892 as the Gooderham & Worts Distillery administrative office. Take in the distinctive exterior, turret and sloping copper roof, then pop around to the western facade overlooking Berczy Park (p68), where a 1980 mural by Canadian artist Derek Michael Besant gives the impression of a drooping open curtain with windows.

## 2 Sky-High Spire

Catch the best Flatiron views on the corner of Front and Church Sts, then continue 200m north to the **Cathedral Church of St James** on King St. Three churches once stood here, but today's neo-Gothic structure was built after Toronto's 1849 fire and was for many years the city's tallest building, with a 93m-tall tower and spire.

## 3 Coffee Stop

St James Park's flower-filled gardens are popular for relaxing, especially when spring blooms are out. A block north, well-established indie-coffee fave **Fahrenheit Coffee** pours strong espresso from Torontonian roaster Omnia.

## 4 A Victorian Beauty

One of Toronto's grandest buildings, **St Lawrence Hall** was created by British architect William Thomas in the 1850s. Corinthian columns, an arched entrance and a green-domed clock tower grace the stone facade of a once-major cultural and social center. It also held gatherings of the abolitionist movement to end the trade of enslaved people. Following years of decay, the building was painstakingly restored in 1967.

## 5 Beloved Market

Heading further south along Jarvis St, you can't miss the twin buildings of **St Lawrence Market** (p64), which face each other on either side of Front St. If it's a weekend, don't miss the famous Saturday farmers market.

## 6 Green Haven

A crop of small, pedestrian-friendly parks extends east along the **Esplanade**, flanked by low-rise, brick apartment buildings dating mostly from the '70s and '80s, when the St Lawrence neighborhood revitalized a swath of industrial land.

## 7 Industrial Hub

A short hop across Parliament Square Park leads to the **Distillery District** (p63), where a lipstick-red steel heart art installation signals your arrival into the revamped 19th-century Gooderham & Worts Distillery. This entire area is now a focus of local creativity, crammed with boutiques, galleries and restaurants.

## EXPERIENCES

### Pop into Toronto's First Post Office
HISTORIC BUILDING

MAP: ① P62 **C2**

An elegant Georgian building on Adelaide St E marks the home of the city's oldest surviving **post office** *(townofyork.com)*, which dates to 1833 and is now protected as a National Historic Site. Still a fully working post office, it also houses a small (donation-based) museum devoted to the early days of Toronto's postal service, originally part of British Royal Mail. You can try your hand at writing a note with a quill, and then mail it on-site.

### Explore with a Local Legend
TOUR

MAP: ② P62 **B3**

Respected Torontonian actor-and-comedian turned historian **Bruce Bell** hosts perhaps the city's most in-demand walking tour *(brucebell tours.ca; tours $30 per person)*, with the Old Town setting the fascinating stage. On a 90-minute, small-group spin that kicks off and wraps up at St Lawrence Market, the district's layers are peeled back with theatrical flair as you take in highlights such as King Edward Hotel or St Lawrence Hall and hear curious snippets about Toronto culture, alongside locals and visitors alike. It's no surprise that Bell's tours get booked up well in advance – plan ahead.

### Pause at Berczy Park Dog Fountain
PARK, FOUNTAIN

MAP: ③ P62 **A3**

Wander over to the lively triangular gardens abutting the famous Flatiron Building (p67) and you're bound to spot people gathering around the two-tier, cast-iron **Berczy Park Dog Fountain**. Said to be one of the city's most-visited sights, it was created as part of Berczy Park's major 2017 makeover by Canadian architect Claude Cormier and depicts 27 water-spouting dogs eyeing a bone (spot the two curious cats, too). Some figures are thought to have been modeled on local canines. If you're here in winter, they'll all be flaunting knitted scarves.

### Explore on Two Wheels
TOUR, CYCLING

MAP: ④ P62 **E4**

With well-established bike paths and easy access to the lakefront, Old Toronto is a great neighborhood to discover by bike. Grab some wheels at Canadian-Dutch–founded **Pedal Toronto** *(pedaltoronto.com; tours from $110)*, based in the thick of the Distillery District – its switched-on team runs a variety of exciting, small-group cycling tours. Options include a twin-market itinerary linking St Lawrence Market with Evergreen Brick Works (p132), or a ride around the Toronto Islands (p58) before taking in the Distillery District's curiosities.

## Relax in Corktown Common  PARK

MAP: **5** P62 **F3**

A former industrial landscape bordering the Don River just east of the Distillery District has been ingeniously reimagined as **Corktown Common** (*toronto. ca*). With artificial marshy areas, shaded paths, sunny meadows and a wave of Carolinian tree species, the 7-hectare park attracts a rich variety of birds and other small-scale wildlife. It's a refreshing spot for a break from the urban buzz (or for catching some fall colors), where you'll be joined by morning dog-walkers and a mostly local crowd on warm evenings.

## Learn About Local History  TOUR

To truly get under the skin of the Old Town – from its millennia-old Indigenous heritage to the 18th-century foundation of the town of York to its modern-day revitalization – it pays to explore with an expert. Led by a team of volunteers, the long-established, nonprofit **Toronto Society of Architects** (*torontosocietyof architects.ca*) organizes spirited two-hour strolls through the St Lawrence district, as seen through an architect's eye (p44). Group tours (*$15 per person*) run from around June to October; private tours (*$295*) are also available.
**Heritage Toronto** (MAP: **6** P62 **B3**; *heritagetoronto.org*) also runs a range of excellent neighborhood walks during warmer months (*$8 per person*), including an art-focused option devoted to the experiences of Toronto's Indigenous Peoples. Schedules change seasonally, so check ahead to find out what's on.

**BEST PERFORMANCE VENUES**

## Young Centre for the Performing Arts

MAP: **7** P62 **F4**

The Distillery District's stunning multi-space arts venue hosts productions by several respected Toronto companies, such as Soulpepper, which celebrates the city's diverse stories and voices (*youngcentre.ca*).

## Reservoir Lounge

MAP: **8** P62 **A3**

Top jazz and blues lounge known for its first-rate live music, nightly performances and classic cocktails (*reservoirlounge.com*).

## Canadian Stage

MAP: **9** P62 **D3**

Also in charge of the summertime Shakespeare performances in High Park (p118), this renowned contemporary theater company has its home stage on Berkeley St (*canadianstage.com*).

## LISTINGS

# Best Places for...

**$** Budget  **$$** Midrange  **$$$** Top End

See p62 for map of locations

## Eating

### Fine Dining

**Restaurant 20 Victoria $$$**
**10** A2

Chef Julie Hyde leads this intimate, Michelin-star kitchen driven by Ontario-sourced produce and seasonal tasting menus. Bar seating for à la carte dining. Booking recommended. *instagram.com/twentyvictoria; 5:30-10pm Wed-Sat*

**Bar Goa $$$**
**11** A2

Inventive plates and tasting menus inspired by contemporary Goan cuisine. Spice-infused cocktails. *bargoa.ca; noon-2:30pm & 4-10pm Tue-Fri, 4-10:30pm Sat, 4-10pm Sun*

**Chef's House $$**
**12** C3

Smart, open-kitchen restaurant. Elegant menus with seasonal ingredients are prepared by culinary students from George Brown College. *thechefshouse.com; 11:30am-1:15pm & 5:30-8:30pm Mon-Fri*

### Italian Flavors

**Gusto 501 $$**
**13** F2

Multilevel King E fave. A fun vibe, rooftop terrace and creative menu of fresh pasta, wood-fire pizzas, house wines and cocktails. *gusto501.com; 5-10pm Mon-Wed, noon-10pm Thu & Sun, noon-11pm Fri & Sat*

**Terroni $$**
**14** A2

Cool southern-Italian spot in a vaulted building. Pizzas topped with homemade ingredients, classic pastas and more. Also runs Spaccio on Sackville St. Branches around Toronto. *terroni.com; 11:30am-9:30pm, to 10pm Fri & Sat*

### Japanese Spots

**Nami $$$**
**15** A2

Behind a neon-blue wave, long-established Nami does sushi and *robata* grill dishes (from smoked salmon to shiitake). It even has its own sake. *namirestaurant.ca; 11:30am-2pm & 5-9pm Mon-Fri, 5-9pm Sat*

**Kinton Ramen $**
**16** D3

Enormous bowls of aromatic ramen with noodles and delicious toppings (veggie options included), from a reliable chain. Great value. *kintonramen.com; 11:30am-9:30pm*

### Burgers & Diners

**Patrician Grill $**
**17** C3

A bright-orange sign marks this family-run diner going strong since the 1950s. Club sandwiches, all-day breakfasts and homemade meatloaf on Fridays. *patriciangrill.com; 7am-3pm Mon-Fri, 8am-2pm Sat*

**Works $$**
**18** B3

Gourmet patties and freshly sizzled fries at this vibrant outpost of the Ottawa-born burger joint. Rooftop patio overlooking the Flatiron. *worksburger.com; 11am-10pm, to 11pm Thu-Sat*

# Drinking

## Breweries & Cocktails

### Mill Street Brewery
 F4

Leading Toronto microbrewer with prize-winning organic craft beer brewed on-site. Lively patio and bar-style menus. *millstreetbrewery.com; 11am-10pm Mon-Sat, 10am-10pm Sun*

### C'est What
 B3

Long-running underground pub for all-natural Ontario craft beers, live music, trivia nights and beer-friendly menus that spotlight St Lawrence Market produce. *cestwhat.com; hours vary*

### Lisbon Hotel
 F2

Try zippy artisanal cocktails and seasonal, European-leaning small plates on a patio opposite Corktown Common or in the lobby-bar-like interior. *lisbonhotel.ca; 5pm-1am Mon-Fri, noon-1am Sat*

## Coffee Culture

### Rooster Coffee House
 D3

Lounge corners and communal seating create a cozy vibe at this popular coffee spot serving roasts and delicious baked goods on King E. Also in Riverdale (p140). *roostercoffeehouse.com; 7am-7pm Mon-Sat, 8am-7pm Sun*

### Mercury Espresso
 F2

Laid-back Corktown cafe where beans from Canadian roasters fuel the brews. Perfect iced coffee. In nearby Leslieville too. *instagram.com/mercuryespresso; 7:30am-4:30pm Mon-Fri, from 8am Sat & Sun*

### Arvo Coffee
 E4

Set in a historic Distillery District building, Arvo is inspired by the coffee scene Down Under. Aussie-sourced brews, brunchy snacks, baked treats. *arvocoffee.com; 7am-6pm Mon-Fri 8am-6pm Sat & Sun*

## Neighborhood Hangouts

### Triple A Bar
 B2

Lively, dog-friendly dive bar opposite St James Park. Street-front patio for warmer months. *tripleabar.ca; 5pm-2am*

### Buvette Pacey
 E1

Montréal-inspired cafe-bar with a terrace down a Corktown side street. Specialty coffee, natural wines, cocktails and local-produce snacks. *buvettepacey.com; 10am-midnight Tue-Sat*

# Shopping

## Fashion & Design

### Peace Collective
 F4

Flagship Distillery store of the Toronto fashion label known for its 'Home Is' collection, community ethos and sports collaborations. *peace-collective.com; 10am-6pm Mon-Fri, to 7pm Sat, 11am-6pm Sun*

### Hoi Bo
 F4

Effortlessly cool, homegrown clothing and accessories. Garments created in-house from natural materials. *hoibo.com; 11am-7pm*

### Blackbird Vintage Finds
 F4

Fun collection of vintage homewares like hand-painted tiles and floral teacups, and locally made artisanal craft pieces, in the Distillery District. *blackbirdvintage.com; 11am-7pm*

### Wildlife Thrift Store
see  B3

Colorful pre-loved-fashion boutique with everything from leather jackets to mix-and-match swimwear. Some proceeds help fund local charities. *wildlifethriftstore.com; 10am-8pm*

# Explore
# Downtown Core & the Village

Looking out on Yonge St, it seems impossible that this dense, bustling urban strip bisecting the city was once a rural road in the town of York. The Downtown Core's southern end is dominated by the sprawling Sankofa Sq and the landmark City Hall and Eaton Centre mall, with heritage buildings hidden around surrounding streets. The Church-Wellesley area (east of Yonge St between Gerrard and Charles Sts) has been the hub of Toronto's LGBTIQ+ scene since the 1980s. Often just called the Village, it puts on a sparkling show with rainbow flags and crosswalks, lively bars and clubs, and one of the world's greatest Pride celebrations.

## Getting Around

**Ⓢ Subway**
Line 1 stops at Queen, Dundas, College and Wellesley, all convenient stations for this large area.

**🚋 Streetcar**
East–west lines 501 (Queen), 505 (Dundas) and 506 (College/Carlton) travel through the Downtown Core.

**🚶 On Foot**
Getting around by walking is a breeze here, with broad main boulevards like Yonge and Queen Sts giving way to quieter sidestreets. The underground PATH network extends up to Dundas St through the Eaton Centre (a tempting option on cold winter days).

★
### THE BEST

**THEATER WORLD**
Elgin & Winter Garden Theatre (p76)

**NIGHTLIFE**
Go dancing in the Village (p80)

**URBAN ARCHITECTURE**
City Hall (p80)

**LGBTIQ+ THEATER**
Buddies in Bad Times (p81)

**FESTIVAL**
Pride Toronto (p81)

City Hall (p80)
COREY WISE/LONELY PLANET

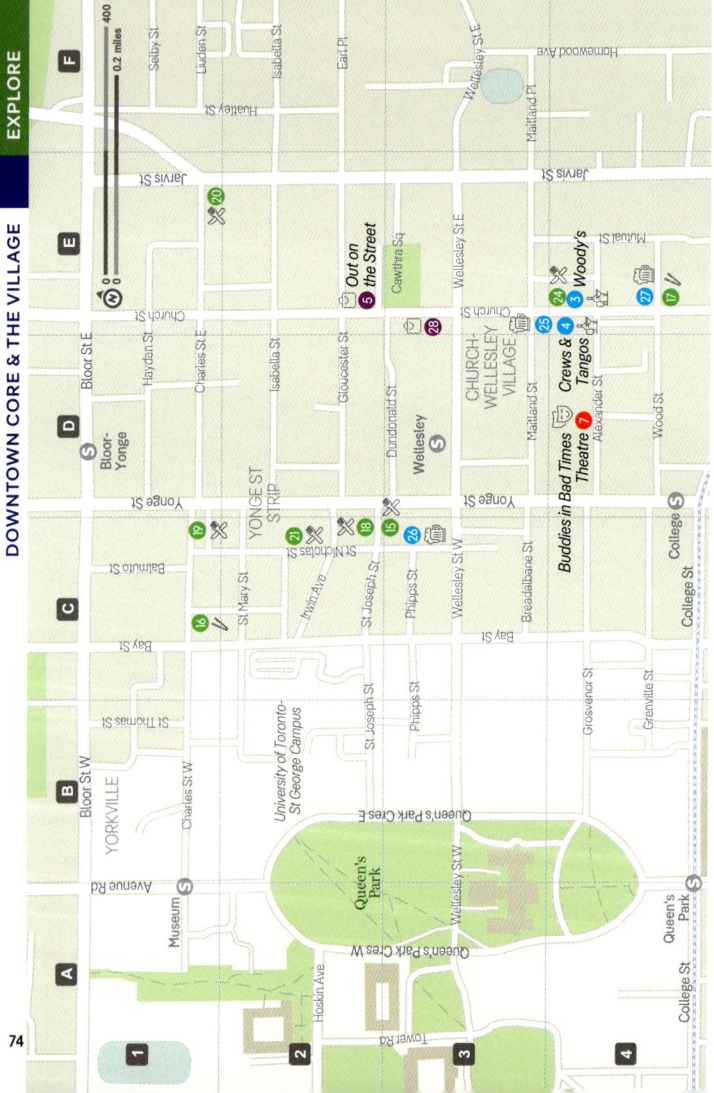

# DOWNTOWN CORE & THE VILLAGE

## EXPLORE

**For more see**
- Top Experiences p76
- Experiences p80
- Eating p84
- Drinking p85
- Shopping p85

### Map labels

- Allan Gardens Conservatory (8)
- Allan Gardens
- Moss Park
- Barbara Ann Scott Park
- Toronto Metropolitan University
- Toronto Coach Terminal
- Toronto General Hospital
- Ed Mirvish Theatre (11)
- Massey Hall (10)
- Elgin & Winter Garden Theatre
- Eaton Centre (9)
- Church of the Holy Trinity (6)
- Nathan Phillips Square (2)
- City Hall (1)
- Textile Museum of Canada (12)

### Streets

- Carlton St
- Gerrard St E
- George St
- Pembroke St
- Dundas St E
- Shuter St
- Queen St E
- Sherbourne St
- Jarvis St
- Mutual St
- Church St
- Dalhousie St
- Bond St
- Victoria St
- Yonge St
- Gould St
- Granby St
- Elm St
- Edward St
- James St
- Albert St
- Bay St
- LaPlante Ave
- Hagerman St
- Elizabeth St
- Centre Ave
- Dundas St W
- Gerrard St W
- University Ave
- Simcoe St
- St Patrick St
- Murray St
- Orde St
- McCaul St
- Yonge & Dundas Sq

75

★ **TOP EXPERIENCE**

# Elgin & Winter Garden Theatre

Rescued from demolition in the 1980s, this is the world's last operating double-decker theater, opened in 1913. Today's wonderful building is part restored masterpiece, part creative extension, and still a working performance venue.

MAP: P74 **D8**

### Elgin Theatre

A long, sparkling lobby greets guests, filled with arched mirrors, stained-glass doors and busts of theater-world greats. The atmospheric, 1538-seat Elgin is tucked into the lower half of the complex. With beautiful deep-red walls and velvet seating, the space functioned as a vaudeville stage from 1913–29, and then as a movie theater. Of particular interest are the hand-beaded lights (based on original designs), sculptures depicting the winemaking god Bacchus (or Dionysus), and the soaring ceiling with intricate floral features (ask about the missing chandelier).

### Winter Garden Theatre

There's bound to be a collective gasp as guides throw open the doors to the Winter Garden Theatre, directly above the Elgin. The most prestigious of the two theaters was designed to feel like a year-round green haven, but lay abandoned for 60 years before being meticulously restored. Much of what remains is original, including the opera boxes and hand-painted wall murals. The ceiling is covered in over 20,000 branches of re-created leaves (in the theater's heyday they were real). The chance to step backstage and glimpse old and new dressing rooms is a fascinating perk.

**PLANNING TIP**
Unless you're catching a live show, the theater is only open to the public via 90-minute guided tour, usually scheduled once or twice weekly. Bookings are essential.

Scan for tour details, tickets and more.

## WALKING TOUR

# Walk the Downtown Core

Exploring this neighborhood is all about taking in the bright lights, bold urban architecture and local public spaces. This is a busy, crowded pocket of the city, so head out early to wander between curious heritage buildings and landmark squares, before checking out the Village, centered on Church St.

| START | END | LENGTH |
|---|---|---|
| Osgoode Hall | Barbara Hall Park | 2.8km; 1hr |

### 1 Legal Hub
Partly hidden behind leafy gardens, **Osgoode Hall** was originally built in the mid-19th century and has been significantly altered since. The structure combines Palladian and Neoclassical features, with an elaborate central facade. Today home to the Law Society of Ontario, it's open to visitors with downloadable audioguides, as well as for weekday tours in summer.

### 2 Civic Square
Just 200m east on Queen St is **Nathan Phillips Square**, where the mammoth City Hall (p80) rises behind the much-photographed 'Toronto' sign. Fans of the hit TV adaptation of Margaret Atwood's novel *The Handmaid's Tale* might recognize City Hall as a filming location.

### 3 Victorian Marvel
Wander east across Bay St to peek at the 1899 **Old City Hall**, an imposing Romanesque-style creation by Toronto architect EJ Lennox. Note the gargoyle carvings and off-center bell tower on the brownstone facade. At the time of writing, there were potential plans to transform the building into a museum.

### 4 Banking Architecture
Stroll 300m east along Queen St, then turn left (north) on Yonge St. Just after passing the fantastic Elgin & Winter Garden Theatre (p76), you'll spot the old **Toronto Dominion Bank Building** at 205 Yonge St, built in the style of a Greek Parthenon in the early 1900s, also by EJ Lennox.

### 5 Bright Lights
Continue 300m north along Yonge St to **Sankofa Square** (p82), officially renamed from Yonge-Dundas Sq in 2024. Often compared to New York's Times Sq, the landmark public space was created in the early 2000s to help revitalize this area. It has water features and enormous billboards and sometimes hosts festivals.

### 6 Hockey History
Walk north to Gould St, then weave east through the vehicle-free grounds of Toronto Metropolitan University to Church St. Around 500m north is **Maple Leaf Gardens**, a 1931 yellow-brick building that for over 60 years was the home of the Toronto Maple Leafs. A major recent redevelopment has transformed it into an athletic center. Also here is the Loblaws' grocery-chain flagship.

### 7 Village Heritage
Head 600m north on Church St through the Village, one of North America's liveliest LGBTIQ+ neighborhoods, to **Barbara Hall Park**. This small green space has an AIDS memorial and a beautiful three-story mural celebrating historical milestones for the LGBTIQ+ community.

## EXPERIENCES

### Admire City Hall
ARCHITECTURE

MAP: ① P74 C7

The imposing, curved twin towers of **City Hall** *(toronto.ca)* rise off Queen St and surround a central flying-saucer-like amphitheater accessed by enormous concrete ramps. Though much-maligned at the time, the building broke new ground when it went up in 1965, marking a major leap for Toronto architecture, and it remains a bold symbol of the city. Finnish architect Viljo Revell was behind the competition-winning design, though he passed away before construction was completed. Stop by the information desk to enquire about self-guided visits. Highlights include a beautiful painting by Anishinaabe artist Norval Morrisseau on the 2nd floor. The annual **Doors Open Toronto** event in May is a great time to visit.

Out the front is **Nathan Phillips Square** (MAP: ② P74 B8), a magnet for food trucks, winter ice-skating, selfies with the 'Toronto' sign, and summer markets, festivals and concerts. In the square's southwest corner sits an Indigenous spirit garden, with a limestone turtle sculpture by Anishinaabe artist Solomon King; it was created in 2024 to draw awareness to the trauma of residential schools in Canada.

### Go Dancing in the Village
NIGHTLIFE

During Toronto's Pride celebrations each June, the Village morphs into an enormous, sparkling street party. At any time of the year, it's a fabulously fun place for relaxing over drinks, catching a drag show or dancing the night away at the LGBTIQ+ clubs.

The outdoor patio at O'Grady's on Church (p85) is a popular place to get started while watching the Village sashay by. Later on, hop over to **Woody's** (MAP: ③ P74 E4), Toronto's best-known gay bar. With over three decades on Church St, it's a packed venue with a dancy atmosphere, where drag queens take to the stage and revelers mill around the slick bar (Sailor) that sits to one side. Another classic after-dark stop is **Crews & Tangos** (MAP: ④ P74 E4; cash-only), with a lively crowd here for the drag acts, cabaret shows and DJ sessions; the setting is a blue-painted brick house, though potential redevelopment plans were in motion at the time of writing. Most places stay open until around 2am or 3am.

Also on Church St, cheeky store **Out on the Street** (MAP: ⑤ P74 E2; *outonthestreet.ca*) has several floors of LGBTIQ+-oriented merch, sex toys and Pride souvenirs. It has been a fixture of the scene since the 1990s.

### Take a Break at the Church of the Holy Trinity CHURCH

MAP: 6 P74 C7

If the hustle and bustle of the Downtown Core start to overwhelm, seek out the oasis-like Trinity Sq hidden away on the west side of the Eaton Centre mall (p82). Here you'll find the Anglican **Church of the Holy Trinity** *(holytrinity.to)*, which was opened in 1847 thanks to an anonymous donor and became the first church in Toronto not to charge parishioners for pews. Today, the Gothic Revival house of worship is notable for welcoming same-sex marriage ceremonies and for its work in forging partnerships with diverse communities across the city. In all, it's a cross between a church, a small concert venue and a community drop-in center. Outside the building is a labyrinth, custom-designed as a quiet, meditative space.

### Dive into LGBTIQ+ Theater PERFORMING ARTS

MAP: 7 P74 D4

The world's oldest LGBTIQ+ theater company has had its permanent home in the Village since the 1990s. Known for its cutting-edge and thought-provoking creations, **Buddies in Bad Times Theatre** *(buddiesinbadtimes.com)* was first launched in 1979 and aims to celebrate a wide range of LGBTIQ+ voices, stories and identities on the stage. The bold, mixed-genre **Rhubarb!** live arts festival in February is a big highlight. Check ahead for what's on and to book tickets. On evenings from Wednesday to Sunday, Buddies throws open its chandelier-lit on-site bar Tallulah's, which also often hosts cabaret, dance nights and other events.

### Stroll Through Allan Gardens PARK, CONSERVATORY

MAP: 8 P74 F5

Wandering into the gorgeous **Allan Gardens Conservatory** *(toronto.ca; free)* feels like discovering a tropical paradise in the thick of the urban jungle, particularly on a cold winter day. A winding indoor botanical garden filled with plants from all over the world awaits within an eye-catching building of cast iron and glass.

---

 PRIDE TORONTO

One of the globe's biggest LGBTIQ+ celebrations kicks off each June with **Pride Toronto** *(pridetoronto.com)*, a monthlong gathering of community events, workshops, shows and festivities (most of them free to attend). Much of the fun revolves around the Village, and the whole event culminates in a rainbow-filled Pride Parade that pulls in around three million revelers. If you're keen to dig deeper into Toronto's LGBTIQ+ heritage and the history of the Village's scene, check for neighborhood tours with Heritage Toronto (p69).

Many visitors make a beeline for the famous Palm House, which dates from 1910; reopened in mid-2025 following a major three-year restoration, it's a lush haven of palms, hibiscus and banana plants. Bring a book if you like and linger on the benches.

The surrounding Allan Gardens park is one of Toronto's oldest, laid out in 1858, and has been an important space for women's movements since its beginnings. This heritage continues in action today, with the park hosting part of the Pride-month **Dyke March**, as well as **Sisters in Spirit** vigils for missing and murdered Indigenous women.

### Browse the Eaton Centre    MALL

MAP: ❾ P74 C7

One of the most-visited attractions in Toronto, the gargantuan **Eaton Centre** *(shops.cadillacfairview.com)* sprawls between Queen St and Sankofa Sq, taking in a sweeping glass-roofed gallery designed by the late German-Canadian architect Eberhard Zeidler. Setting foot inside Downtown's largest shopping mall is a sensory overload, from the raft of international retailers to the *Flight Stop* art installation near the southern entrance, featuring a flock of suspended fiberglass geese created by the Canadian artist Michael Snow.

On cold winter days, the whole space offers a bright retreat from the elements, especially during the festive season when people pack in to see the twinkling Christmas tree and regular snow shows. Drop by in the morning on a weekday for a more relaxed experience with fewer crowds.

### Feel the Music    LIVE MUSIC

MAP: ❿ P74 D8

A leading Canadian music venue since the 1890s, **Massey Hall** *(masseyhall.mhrth.com)* is a classic of Toronto's fired-up music scene and counts everyone from Joni Mitchell to Montserrat Caballé to Luciano Pavarotti among its former guests. Now a National Historic Site, it has recently seen a massive restoration revive its original 100-plus stained-glass

---

### RENAMING SANKOFA SQUARE

In 2024, Toronto authorities voted in favor of renaming the former Yonge-Dundas Sq to Sankofa Sq. The move is part of a wider, ongoing conversation about renaming places in Toronto associated with the 18th-century politician Henry Dundas for his perceived links to the trade of enslaved people. At the time of writing, plans had been approved for Dundas subway station to be renamed TMU station, and there were also some calls for Dundas St to be renamed.

windows, plaster ceiling and red-brick exterior, which now stands between glinting skyscrapers just off Queen St E. Gordon Lightfoot played his 170th show here when it relaunched in 2021. Check for upcoming shows to experience this much-loved heritage space in all its musical glory.

A few doors away fronting both Yonge and Victoria Sts is the acclaimed **Ed Mirvish Theatre** (MAP: 11 P74 D7; *mirvish.com*), a grand 1920s-era vaudeville hall that now hosts musical extravaganzas. Originally called Pantages Theatre, it has been through several incarnations since its founding, and was renamed in 2011 in honor of the late Ed Mirvish, a well-loved Toronto businessman, philanthropist and patron of the arts.

### Take a Guided Walk          TOUR

The Downtown Core has long been a hub for civic engagement in public spaces and a place where the city's layered heritage collides with its modern-day identity. Learn all about some of the key conversations happening in contemporary Toronto on a three-hour guided stroll with the **Tour Guys** *(tourguys.ca)*, whose Past, Present & Future Walking Tour combines spending time in the Old Town with some key Downtown stops such as City Hall (p80), Sankofa Sq and the Toronto Metropolitan University.

### Find Fabrics at the Toronto Textile Museum   MUSEUM

MAP: 12 P74 B7

Tucked into a condo tower, the small **Textile Museum of Canada** *(textilemuseum.ca)* has exhibits drawing on its permanent collection of more than 13,000 items from Latin America, Africa, Europe, Southeast Asia and India, as well as contemporary Canada. Workshops teach batik making, weaving, knitting and all manner of needlecraft. At the time of writing, the museum was closed for renovations but expected to open late 2025. Check its website for the latest.

## LISTINGS

# Best Places for...

💲 Budget   💲💲 Midrange   💲💲💲 Top End

See p74 for map of locations

## Eating

### Southeast Asian Cooking

**Som Tum Jinda** 💲💲
**13** E5

Vibrant, mural-filled restaurant known for its Isan-style *som tum* (papaya salad) dishes. Other northeast-Thai treats include deliciously spiced noodles, meaty stir-fries and several vegan plates. *somtum jinda.ca; hours vary*

**Salad King** 💲
**14** D6

Generous salads, yes, but also large bowls of steaming Thai curries, wok-fried noodles and spicy soups. Popular with a student crowd, and also has a location on Queen St W. *saladking.com; 11:30am-9pm Mon-Fri, noon-9pm Sat, noon-8:30pm Sun*

**Lao Lao Bar** 💲💲
**15** C3

Beautifully designed restaurant with bar seating, umbrella-shaped lamps and Laotian cooking, including great-value set lunch menus and rices served in slices of pineapple. *laolaobar.com; hours vary*

### Japanese Kitchens

**Okonomi House** 💲
**16** C1

Long-running, fuss-free place specializing in authentic *okonomiyaki*, savory Japanese cabbage pancakes filled with meat, seafood or vegetables. *instagram.com/okonomihouse; noon-3pm & 5-9pm Tue-Sat*

**Afuri Ramen** 💲💲
**17** E4

Shared tables, bar seats and industrial vibes fill this Japan-born Church-Wellesley spot loved for its ramen made with house-crafted noodles and yuzu broth. *afuriramen.com; 11am-10:30pm*

### Cool Cafes

**Nabulu Coffee** 💲
**18** C2

A repurposed townhouse is the setting for a cozy vintage-feel cafe where a stylish crowd enjoys fresh pastries and cakes alongside rotating beans from local roasters. *nabulucoffee.ca; 8am-11pm*

**7 West Cafe** 💲💲
**19** C1

Three floors of atmospheric lighting, framed nudes, wooden church pews and jaunty ceiling angels go with tasty pizzas, pastas, sandwiches and 24-hour breakfasts. *7westcafe.com; 24hr*

**Rooster Coffee House** 💲
**20** E1

Pick up a cheddar scone and a strong flat white to enjoy on the Jarvis St patio of this popular indie cafe originally started in the East End. *roostercoffeehouse.com; 7am-7pm*

### Vegan Spots

**Avelo** 💲💲💲
**21** C2

Seasonal menus change daily at this creative, plant-based fine-dining address hidden in a heritage building. Upstairs there's a cocktail bar with light bites. *avelorestaurant.com; 5-11pm*

### Local Classics & Pizza

#### Senator Restaurant ❸❸❸
 D7

Established in the 1940s and still going strong, the Senator has an Art Deco feel and menus fueled by locally sourced produce – grilled asparagus, fresh meatloaf, daily desserts. *thesenator.com; 5-8pm Tue-Fri, 9:30am-2pm & 5-8pm Sat, 9:30am-2pm Sun*

#### Golden Diner Family Restaurant ❸
❷❸ E5

New York–style diner keeping things pleasingly old school in the heart of the city, with original booths and all-day breakfasts stacked with eggs, bacon and home fries. *7am-8pm*

#### North of Brooklyn ❸❸
❷❹ E4

New York–style thin-crust pizzas with delicious toppings like truffle or pepperoni are the thing at this small, casual Church St fave. *11:30am-10pm Sun-Wed, to 11pm Thu-Sat*

# Drinking

## Pubs & Breweries

### O'Grady's On Church
 E3

The Village's best patio? Head to this fun Irish pub for drinks in the sun and bar-style food (burgers, salads), along with fabulous drag shows and, on Wednesdays, Dirty Bingo. *10am-2am; instagram.com/ogradysonchurch*

### Bar Volo
 C3

A rotating selection of 26 craft brews on tap (including house-brewed ales) draws beer-lovers to Bar Volo, just off Yonge St. Pair them with Italian snacks like burrata with pesto. *barvolo.com; 11:30am-1am Sun-Thu, to 2am Fri & Sat*

### Hair of the Dog
 E4

Relaxed neighborhood pub at the south end of the Village, at its best on the two-floor patio during warmer months. Pick from Ontario craft beers, burger-like sandwiches and more. *hairofthedogpub.ca; 10:30am-midnight Sun-Thu, to 1am Fri & Sat*

# Shopping

## Books & Records

### Dead Dog Records
❷❽ E3

A small, locally loved used-record store with a great selection of vinyls, CDs, cassette tapes and merch from long-past concerts. There's another branch on Bloor St. *deaddogrecords.com; noon-7pm Tue-Sat, to 5pm Sun*

### Ben McNally
❷❾ E8

Browse for your next read at this warm, independent bookshop, which also hosts author talks, book launches and other literary events. *benmcnallybooks.com; 10am-5pm Mon-Sat*

# Explore
# Chinatown, Kensington Market, Queen West & Little Italy

Toronto's multicultural identity is on full show in the side-by-side neighborhoods of Chinatown and Kensington Market, both shaped over the years by waves of migration. Chinatown straddles Spadina Ave, taking in the unmissable Art Gallery of Ontario, late-night eats, dim sum treats and small grocers. Kensington has an easy-going energy, vintage boutiques and globe-trotting kitchens. South of Chinatown, Queen West encompasses a busy swath centered on shop-lined Queen St, with brightly muraled alleys and a thriving live-music scene. The lively area around College St W is Little Italy, home to some of Toronto's trendiest bars and restaurants.

## Getting Around

 **Subway**
Line 1 has several convenient stops along University Ave on the east side of Chinatown.

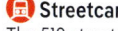 **Streetcar**
The 510 streetcar runs north-south along Spadina Ave. Also handy are east-west streetcars 505 (Dundas St), 506 (College St) and 501 (Queen St).

 **Walking**
With broad sidewalks, you can't beat exploring on foot here.

**Kensington Market (p94)**
SPIROVIEW INC/SHUTTERSTOCK

★
## THE BEST

**MUSEUM**
Art Gallery of Ontario (p90)

**FOOD SCENE** Taste Your Way Around Town (p94)

**VINTAGE SHOPPING**
Kensington Market (p94)

**STREET ART**
Graffiti Alley (p95)

**COCKTAIL HOUR**
Bar Pompette (p96)

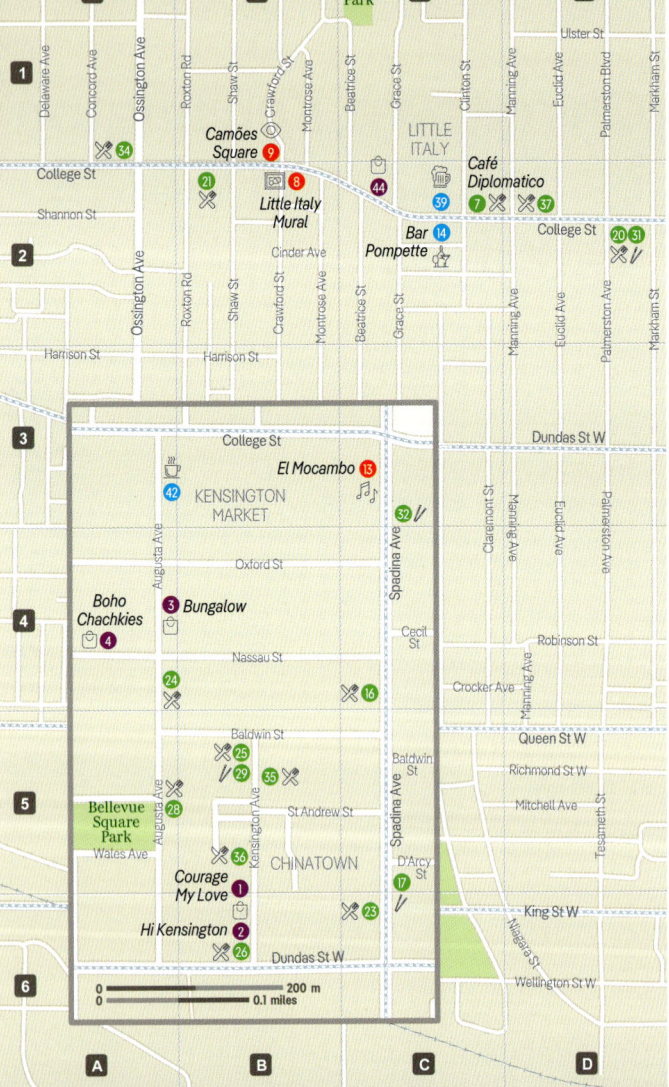

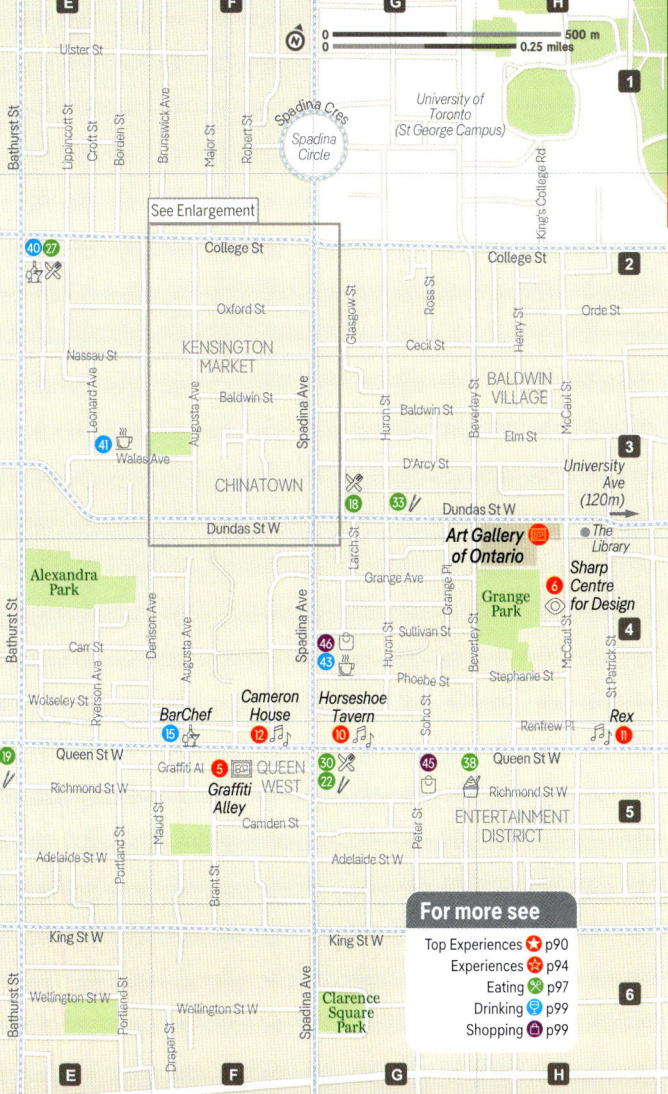

★ **TOP EXPERIENCE**

# Art Gallery of Ontario

A work of art itself inside and out, the Art Gallery of Ontario (AGO) is a spectacular building reminiscent of a crystal ship. It holds a remarkable collection of more than 120,000 works spread across several architecturally eye-catching wings, making it one of Canada's finest museums.

MAP P88 **H3**

**PLANNING TIP**
Volunteer-led pop-up art chats are often available on a drop-in basis. The AGO has great offerings for kids, including roving arts carts and an experiential center.

Scan for prices, opening hours and tour information.

### Architecture & Design

The AGO building itself is as notable as the works of art inside. The original building, dating to 1900, has been renovated and expanded several times. Perhaps the most striking update was the 2008 redesign by revered Canadian architect Frank Gehry. The almost dreamlike new elements include the stunning entrance, a curving ship-like glass wall that reflects the Victorian houses across the way; the Walker Court's spiraling baroque staircase, a wooden curlicue rising through a glass ceiling; and the breathtaking Galleria Italia, its tall, organic wooden beams and floor-to-ceiling windows calling to mind the hull of a ship. Don't miss the skyline views from the lofty, spiral Barnacle Staircase overlooking Grange Park.

### Indigenous Art

The AGO's ever-growing Indigenous art collection spans the centuries, with a sharp focus on artwork from North America, and Canada's largest collection of art by Aboriginal and Torres Strait Islander peoples. Keep an eye out for several vibrant works by renowned Anishinaabe painter Norval Morrisseau and *The Wisdom of the Universe* by prominent Métis artist Christi Belcourt.

BERT HOFERICHTER/ALAMY

## Other Highlights

The intense drama of Canada's vast landscapes is beautifully evoked by the collection Group of Seven works, whose highlights range from Tom Thomson's depictions of the Algonquin lakes region to Lawren S Harris' cool blue paintings of the Canadian North, all on Level 2. Also here is the Henry Moore Sculpture Gallery, the world's largest collection of this monumental artist's works. Another must-see is Yayoi Kusama's *Infinity Mirrored Room – Let's Survive Forever*. The galleries on Level 1 are devoted to European art, taking in pieces by Monet, Degas and other greats. As you explore, take advantage of in-gallery leaflets and QR codes diving into detail for particular pieces.

**QUICK BREAK**
The AGO has a bistro serving seasonal menus and an espresso bar in the light-filled Galleria Italia. Or pop over to **The Library** *(thelibrary specialtycoffee. com)* for third-wave brews.

# WALKING TOUR

# Chinatown & Kensington Market

Filled with life any time of day (or night), these two districts surrounding busy Spadina Ave make up one of Toronto's most atmospheric pockets. Explore their story on a leisurely walk linking open-air art, local shops and lesser-known corners.

| START | END | LENGTH |
|---|---|---|
| Queen West | Augusta Ave | 2km; 45min |

92

### 1. Street-Art Hub

Begin at the well-connected intersection of Queen St W and Spadina Ave, in the heart of mural-filled **Queen West**. Walk 500m north along Spadina Ave. Chinatown quickly emerges with vegetable counters piled high outside grocery stores and a sprinkling of restaurants serving dumplings, noodles, roast duck and other classics.

### 2. Welcome to Chinatown

At the junction of Spadina Ave and Dundas St, pause overlooking the Spadina streetcar tracks to see **Gateway** – a duo of bright-red sculptures by artist Millie Chen, one each on the north and south sides of the intersection. Four mythical creatures are intertwined in the shape of the ancient Chinese characters for 'gateway' – dragon, phoenix, monkey king and unicorn.

### 3. Ornamental Square

Turn right (east) on Dundas St and stroll one block along to Huron St, where a small section has been pedestrianized as **Huron Square**. The plaza's intricate red-themed decoration and seating space take inspiration from illuminated Chinese Zodiac lanterns, and are joined by a benevolent bronze Qilin sculpture.

### 4. Feline Art

Double back to Spadina, cross the street and wander 200m north. At the corner of Spadina and St Andrew St, spot **Cat on a Chair**, a lofty 1990s sculpture by Shirley Yanover and David Hlynsky marking the point where Chinatown gives way to Kensington Market. The attentive cat, poised with a paw up, recalls a time when felines scurried around nearby market stalls.

### 5. Vintage Haven

Walking west along St Andrew St you'll soon pass the 1930 Anshei Minsk Synagogue, still in use today. Then turn left (south) on to colorful **Kensington Ave**, where rows of Victorian houses now host a wave of vintage and secondhand shops (p94).

### 6. Doughnut Time

Heading north on Kensington Ave, small, market-like brick buildings replace the Victorian homes and bold street art bursts on to the walls. Make a tiny detour right (east) on Baldwin St for a light, sugary treat at popular **Dipped Donuts**, perhaps a hazelnut crunch or apple fritter.

### 7. Garden on Wheels

Head west back along Baldwin St to Augusta Ave and turn right (north) for another 200m. From May to October, you can't miss the **Kensington Market Garden Car**, a muraled vehicle transformed into a tiny green space with plants growing out of it at the junction of Augusta Ave and Oxford St. Classic Kensington Market.

## EXPERIENCES

### Taste Your Way Around Town     TOUR

The best way to dive into the interlinked backstory of Chinatown and Kensington Market is through their thrilling, distinctive culinary scenes. Sizzling noodles, pillowy dumplings, herby banh mi, weekend dim sum and other treats pull food lovers into Chinatown, while Kensington Market's richly diverse cuisines have been shaped by the different communities that have settled here over the years (see below).

Popular **Culinary Adventure Co** *(culinaryadventureco.com; adult/child $129/124)* runs terrific three-hour food tours hopping between the two districts, which weave in chapters from their intriguing histories and might combine, for example, steaming fresh dumplings, rich Jamaican patties and Ontario-made cheeses.

**Chopsticks & Forks** *(chopsticksandforks.com; adult/child $119/104)* delves into Kensington Market with two tempting three-hour food romps focusing on multiculturalism and fusion cooking, with stops at independent retailers and plenty of historical, cultural and architectural insight. Arrive hungry.

### Go Thrifting in Kensington Market     SHOPPING

Fashion lovers with a taste for vintage will want to spend a few hours thrifting around Kensington Market, home to a vibrant pre-loved-clothing scene for decades. Kensington Ave has several longtime favorites set inside pastel-walled Victorian-era houses. Still run by the same family, **Courage My Love** (MAP:  P88 **B5**; *instagram.com/cececourage*) opened in the 1970s in a blue-fronted home and draws stylish regulars (celebrities included) with its beautiful collections of lace dresses, colorful glassware, retro shirts and handpicked jewelry. It's all very chic at neighboring

---

### KENSINGTON MARKET HISTORY

A National Historic Site of Canada since 2006, multicultural Kensington Market owes its identity to various waves of migration since the early 20th century. Its modern-day origins can be traced back to British and Irish immigrants putting down roots with Victorian homes on formerly agricultural land. The district morphed into a market in the first half of the 20th century, as Jewish immigrants from Europe and Russia arrived, often working in the nearby Garment District. The 1960s saw an influx of new arrivals from China, the Caribbean and India, while the influence of many Latin American communities is felt today in the neighborhood's tantalizing culinary offerings.

**Hi Kensington** (MAP: ❷ P88 **B6**; *instagram.com/hi.kensington .vintage*), which stocks vintage slip dresses, crop tops, bags, jewelry and other treats, plus its own contemporary designs made using secondhand fabrics.

At **Bungalow** (MAP: ❸ P88 **A4**; *bungalow.to*) on Augusta Ave, you might spy mid-Century Modern tableware, denim jackets, retro sunglasses and pillbox hats, along with current clothing. A few doors away on Nassau St, **Boho Chachkies** (MAP: ❹ P88 **A4**; *bohochachkies.com*) started life as a pop-up and has grown into a 28-vendor, market-vibe hub.

## Walk Down Graffiti Alley  STREET ART

MAP: ❺ P88 **F5**

A back lane tucked between Queen St W and Richmond St has grown into one of Toronto's most popular places to create and see street art. Across three blocks from Spadina Ave to Portland St, **Graffiti Alley** (officially Rush La) bursts into color with magnificent murals, some of which sweep across entire buildings. Among many must-sees is prolific local artist uber5000's humorous *Toronto Tribute* mural, an enormous tongue-in-cheek work showing off the CN Tower, a crane and even a red helicopter.

If you're keen to dig a little deeper, **Tour Guys** (*tourguys.ca*) offers excellent, pay-what-you-like guided walks that go well beyond Graffiti Alley to discover Queen West's celebrated street-art scene. Engaging guides dive into the history of street art in Toronto and its 1980s New York–influenced origins. Along the way you'll learn about key artists on the scene today and uncover hidden pieces, tricky to find without an expert's eye. Or check out **StreetARToronto** (*streetartoronto.ca*) for self-guided street-art maps.

## Spot an Architecture Landmark  ARCHITECTURE

MAP: ❻ P88 **H4**

While wandering across Grange Park on the south side of the Art Gallery of Ontario (p90), it's impossible to miss the much-talked-about **Sharp Centre for Design** (*ocadu.ca*). Part of OCAD University, the dramatic structure resembles a gigantic spotted table-top floating above the city on diagonal primary-colored steel-pipe legs, with several earlier red-brick buildings huddled underneath. It was designed by British architect Will Alsop in the mid-2000s and became a controversial yet prize-winning game-changer for contemporary Toronto architecture. There's a great view of the building backed by the CN Tower from McCaul St.

## Wander Through Little Italy  NEIGHBORHOOD

In the late 19th and early 20th centuries, a wave of Italian immigrants arrived in Toronto, many settling first in the densely populated neighborhood of the Ward, then gradually moving west into what is now **Little Italy** (the area around College St W between Bathurst St and Ossington Ave). Later in the 20th century, other communities settled here too, including Portuguese families, and today the area has a strong multicultural identity.

Wandering along College St, trendy food spots and creative bars mingle with traditional pizza counters and long-established classics like **Café Diplomatico** (MAP: ❼ P88 C2; *cafediplomatico.ca*), founded in 1968 and a pioneer of outdoor patio dining in Toronto. A striking **Little Italy mural** (MAP: ❽ P88 B2) adorns the junction of College and Crawford Sts, while across the road **Camões Square** (MAP: ❾ P88 B1) commemorates the area's Portuguese history. Even Italian-French actress Sophia Loren is depicted at College and Grace Sts. Held in June for around 25 years, the **Taste of Little Italy** festival *(tolittleitaly.com)* is a fun time to be here.

### Catch a Concert at the Horseshoe Tavern     LIVE MUSIC

A Toronto institution tracing its roots to 1947, Queen West's **Horseshoe Tavern** (MAP: ❿ P88 G5; *horseshoetavern.com*) still plays a crucial role in the development of local indie rock. This place oozes a history of good times and classic performances. There are shows most days, so see what's on, or just come for a beer and check it out.

Several other of Toronto's finest live-music venues await nearby on Queen St W and Spadina Ave, including outstanding jazz-and-blues spot, the **Rex** (MAP: ⓫ P88 H5; *therex.ca*); intimate mural-adorned concert space **Cameron House** (MAP: ⓬ P88 F5; *thecameron.com*); and neon-signed **El Mocambo** (MAP: ⓭ P88 C3; *elmocambo.com*), where the Rolling Stones performed and recorded a secret show in 1977.

### Hop Between Cocktail Hot Spots     NIGHTLIFE

These interconnected neighborhoods are home to some of the city's most creative cocktail bars, making the area a tempting destination for evening drinks. Wherever you pick, arrive early or prepare to queue. **Bar Pompette** (MAP: ⓮ P88 C2; *pompette.ca*) is an elegantly understated Parisian bar that just happens to be in Little Italy; it's always packed until late with people sipping inventive, elegant cocktails crafted with housemade ingredients. Over on Queen West, swish **BarChef** (MAP: ⓯ P88 F5; *barchef.com*) is an intimate oasis where you'll hear 'oohs' and 'aahs' as cutting-edge drinks emerge from the moodily lit bar.

# LISTINGS

# Best Places for...

$ Budget  $$ Midrange  $$$ Top End

**See p88** for map of locations

## Eating

### Dim Sum & Noodles

**Rol San** $$
 C4

There's often a line for delectable all-day dim sum at this third-generation-owned Spadina staple. Dreamy handmade dumplings come with house chilli sauce. *instagram.com/rolsan.to; 10am-midnight Sun-Thu, to 3am Fri & Sat*

**Swatow** $
17 C5

Small, family-owned, cash-only classic going strong for four decades and catering to a loyal Chinatown crowd (lines likely). Cantonese menus include fiery noodles. *swatowrestauranttoronto.com; 11am-10:30pm Sun-Thu, to 11:30pm Fri & Sat*

**House of Gourmet** $
18 G3

A popular, fluorescent-bulb-lit restaurant specializing in fresh Hong Kong–style congee, noodles and BBQ among hundreds of dishes. Try the wonton-brisket-noodle soup. *houseofgourmet.ca; 10am-1am Sun-Thu, to 2am Fri & Sat*

**Wonton Hut** $
19 E5

The minimal Queen West branch of a Markham fave does fresh pillowy wontons filled with pork and shrimp and served with thin noodles in a fragrant broth. *wontonhut.ca; noon-9pm*

### Tapas & Spanish

**Bar Raval** $$
 D2

A wavy, Gaudí-inspired bar dazzles at Toronto's most buzz-worthy tapas spot, where bold sherries and vermouths accompany lightly creative bites. Great patio. *thisisbarraval.com; 1pm-1am*

**Bar Isabel** $$$
21 B2

Delicious contemporary Spanish dishes are best enjoyed for sharing at this College St hot spot. Try jamón croquettes or grilled octopus. *barisabel.com; 5-11pm Sun-Fri, noon-11pm Sat*

### Pho & Banh Mi

**Cà Phê Rang** $$
 G5

Understated, popular Spadina spot dishing up super-fresh banh mi (vegan included) and pho bowls big enough to share. *capherang.ca; 11am-9pm Sun-Thu, to 11pm Fri & Sat*

**Nguyen Huong** $
 C6

Cheap and delicious filled Vietnamese sandwiches and crunchy spring rolls are the order of the day. Cash only, takeout only. *nguyenhuong.ca; 8am-7pm*

### Mexican Cuisine

**Gus Tacos** $
 A4

Classic, unfussy corn tacos, burritos and quesadillas are the stars at this Kensington hit. Veggies will love the fresh-cheese and

avocado tacos. *gustacos.com*; 11am-9pm

### Seven Lives $
**25** B5

Pop-up taqueria turned laid-back, mostly take-out place. Baja-style tacos filled with spicy shrimp, fish or chorizo and potato. *sevenlivesto.ca*; noon-7pm

### El Rey Mezcal $$
**26** B6

Kensington Market go-to, perfect for a zingy margarita on the patio and bites like fresh guac and al pastor tacos. *elreybar.com*; 5pm-midnight Mon-Thu, from noon Sat & Sun

### Quetzal $$$
**27** E2

Elevated Mexican flavors get the Michelin-star treatment with ambitious open-flamed cooking, tasting menus and à la carte dining. *quetzaltoronto.com*; 6-10pm Wed-Sun

## Creative Hot Spots

### Grey Gardens $$$
**28** A5

Stylish bistro-vibe restaurant in Kensington Market with carefully curated wines, rotating globally inspired menus and bar seating overlooking an open kitchen. *greygardens.ca*; 5-10pm Mon-Sat

### Sunnys Chinese $$$
**29** B5

Kensington Market sensation with a speakeasy feel, hidden down a shop hallway. Exquisite sharing-style dishes spotlight flavors from across China. *sunnyschinese.com*; 5-10:30pm Wed-Sat, to 10pm Sun

### Alo $$$
 G5

A shining, Michelin-awarded star of the Toronto food scene, renowned for chef Patrick Kriss' season-fired, French-inspired tasting menus. Also has less formal bar dining. *alorestaurant.com*; 5pm-midnight Tue-Sat

### DaiLo $$
**31** D2

Chic Asian brasserie serving French-meets-Chinese dishes in Little Italy courtesy of chef Nick Liu. *dailoto.com*; 5-10pm Mon-Thu & Sun, to 2am Fri & Sat

## Delicious Dumplings

### Mother's Dumplings $
**32** C3

Traditional Chinatown kitchen for plump, juicy dumplings prepared using authentic recipes passed down for generations. Always busy. *mothersdumplings.com*; 11:30am-9:30pm

### Yummy Yummy Dumplings $
**33** G3

Family-owned basement dumpling house with a strong following for its authentically tasty fresh fillings. *yummy-yummy-dumplings.res-menu.com*; 11am-9pm Thu-Tue

## Caribbean Flavors

### Conejo Negro $$$
 A1

Innovative Caribbean, Creole and Latin fusion draws crowds to this stylish College spot with a vibey patio, inventive cocktails and sharing-style plates. *conejonegrotoronto.com*; 5-10pm Tue-Thu, to 11pm Fri & Sat

### Rasta Pasta $$
**35** B5

Jamaican and Italian flavors combine at a popular Kensington kitchen where two-day-marinated chicken is served in a panini. Also at Waterworks Food Hall (p45). *eatrastapasta.ca*; 11am-7pm Tue-Sat, to 6pm Sun

## Sweet Treats

### Fika
 B5

Turquoise Victorian house turned cozy Scandi-vibe cafe, for home-roasted coffee and freshly baked cinnamon buns on the patio. *fika.ca; 10:30am-5pm Sun-Thu, to 6pm Sat*

### Cafe Belém
 D2

Indoor greenery, a buzzy atmosphere and trays of oven-fresh *pastéis de nata* (custard tarts) at this gorgeously designed Portuguese cafe on College St. *cafebelem.ca; 8am-6pm Wed-Sat, to 4pm Sun*

### Good Behaviour
 G5

This bright, casual spot on Queen West is loved for creative sub sandwiches and original ice-cream flavors. *goodbehaviourto.ca; 10am-10pm*

## Drinking

### Beers & Dive Bars

### Birreria Volo
 C2

Tightly packed craft-beer hall from the team behind Downtown's hit Bar Volo (p85), pouring mostly Ontario-sourced brews, plus Italian wines and snacky bites. *birreriavolo.com; hours vary*

### Sneaky Dee's
 E2

Little Italy's graffiti-clad Sneaky Dee's has years of history, cheap beers, live music and a popular trivia night. *sneakydees.com; 11am-3am Mon-Fri, from 10am Sat & Sun*

### Coffee Culture

### Made Rite Coffee
 E3

Cool retro-feel cafe with a laid-back patio on a quiet Kensington corner. Specialty brews and savory breakfast sandwiches. *instagram.com/maderitecoffee; 8am-4pm Mon-Sat*

### Pamenar
 A3

All-day Kensington cafe-bar with a low-key atmosphere, morning coffees, evening G&Ts and a lovely tucked-away patio. *instagram.com/pamenar_km; hours vary*

### Dark Horse Espresso
 G4

Excellent coffee in a tall-ceilinged lounge overlooking the Chinatown action, perfect for people-watching, chatting or getting work done. *darkhorseespresso.com; 7am-7pm Mon-Fri, from 8am Sat & Sun*

## Shopping

### Art & Crafts

### Arts Market
 C2

Intriguing multi-vendor store where a collective of local artists and artisans sell handmade jewelry, original cards and fragrant botanical candles. *artsmarket.ca; 11am-6pm*

### Books & Vinyl

### Flying Books
45 G5

Indie publisher stocking a wide range of titles at its Queen West store, which doubles as a cafe-bar. Also on College St. *flyingbooks.ca; 8am-9pm Sun-Thu, to 10pm Fri & Sat*

### Sonic Boom
46 G4

The largest indie record store in Canada, with rows upon rows of new and used vinyl, CDs and even cassettes. *sonicboommusic.com; 11am-8pm*

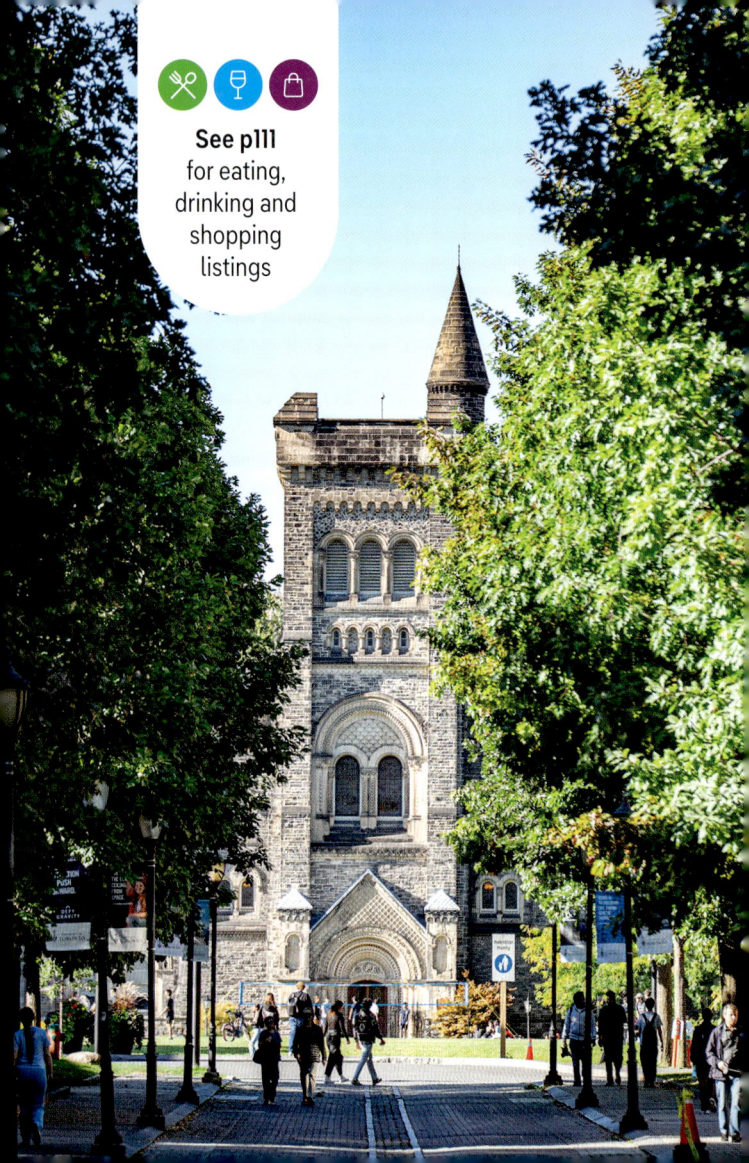

# Explore
# Yorkville, the Annex & University of Toronto

Centered on always-busy Bloor St, between Yonge St and Avenue Rd, Yorkville is Toronto's high-end hub of shopping, dining and accommodations, and also hosts several top-tier museums. This compact area was originally a separate town and still retains a delightful village-like feel with its pedestrian-friendly streets, interconnected squares and Victorian homes. Sprawling to the west is the Annex, a largely residential district with a strong student population and a big food-and-drink scene, especially along Bloor. South of Bloor St lie the historical grounds of the University of Toronto, bordered to the west by Harbord Village neighborhood, home to laid-back cafes, restaurants and shops.

## Getting Around

 **Subway**
Lines 1 and 2 intersect at Bloor–Yonge, St George and Spadina stations, all on Bloor St. Line 2 runs east–west along Bloor; Bay, Bathurst and Christie are convenient stops too, as is Museum on Line 1.

 **Streetcar & Bus**
The 506 streetcar travels along College St, while the 510 runs along Spadina Ave. Bus 94A goes east–west along Harbord and Wellesley Sts.

Much of this area is pedestrian-friendly, especially Yorkville and the University of Toronto.

**University College (p107), University of Toronto**
ERMAN GUNES/SHUTTERSTOCK

### THE BEST

**MUSEUM** Royal Ontario Museum (p104)

**INDIGENOUS CULTURES** Native Canadian Centre of Toronto (p108)

**NEIGHBORHOOD WALK** University of Toronto (p106)

**ARCHITECTURE** Casa Loma (p108)

**FILM SCENE** Hot Docs (p110)

103

★ **TOP EXPERIENCE**

# Royal Ontario Museum

One of the largest museums in North America, the ROM wows visitors with galleries of fossils, artifacts, art and hands-on exhibits. The setting is a fascinating amalgam of old and new, with original 20th-century heritage buildings contrasting with the shard-like 2007 Crystal extension.

MAP P102 **F4**

**PLANNING TIP**
Free, 45-minute docent-led tours run daily; check schedules ahead. Admission is free on the third Tuesday evening each month; avoid the rush by arriving later in the session.

Scan for opening hours, tour details and other information.

### Highlights of the ROM

The ROM's full collection takes in a staggering 18 million objects meaning there's a lot to explore, so allow plenty of time and have a few must-sees in mind. The building itself is a visual spectacle, starting with the brilliant **rotunda ceiling** (pictured) in the Beaux Arts main hall (next to the Queen's Park entrance). Against a gold backdrop of Venetian mosaics, its myriad patterns and symbols evoke the breadth of the museum's collection.

Many visitors head directly up to the **Age of Dinosaurs** galleries on Level 2, which are crammed with dinosaur skeletons from the Jurassic to Cretaceous periods. Most were uncovered across North America, especially in Alberta. On Level 3, the Africa-focused galleries include the famous collection of **Egyptian mummies**, presented with a sensitive display that evokes the human stories behind them. Other highlights are the Chinese temple art galleries, wide-ranging Korean art collection and superb printed textiles.

### First Peoples Art & Culture Gallery

An unmissable space on Level 1, this remarkable gallery is devoted to the cultures, arts and worldviews of Canada's Indigenous Peoples, from

ALWAYSSUNNYALWAYSREAL/SHUTTERSTOCK

pre-European times to the present day. Developed in collaboration with Indigenous advisers, the 1000-piece collection takes in birch-bark canoes, ceremonial clothing and traditional beadwork, as well as rotating exhibits.

### Family-Friendly Fun

The museum offers an excellent program of family-friendly activities, including the play-focused **WonderWorks** area, where children can get hands-on with dinosaur models, enjoy age-based books in the reading corner and dive into other learning activities. Kids will also be thrilled by the chance to walk through a re-created Jamaican **bat cave**, where eerie sounds echo all around you (no real bats though).

**QUICK BREAK**
The ROM has a relaxed lobby cafe with light bites at basement level, **Druxy's ROM Café**. Otherwise, walk a few minutes over to Trattoria Nervosa (p111) or the Oxley pub (p113) in Yorkville.

# WALKING TOUR

# University of Toronto

Beginning with one of the city's unmissable museums, this neighborhood stroll combines a touch of glamorous Yorkville with the University of Toronto's leafy, expansive home base. Along the way, discover quiet traffic-free spaces, several centuries of urban architecture and broad green oases.

| START | END | LENGTH |
|---|---|---|
| Royal Ontario Museum | Found Coffee | 2.5km; 45min |

### 1 Must-See Museum

The **Royal Ontario Museum** (p104) makes a bold statement on busy Bloor St, combining original early-20th-century heritage buildings with Daniel Libeskind's prismatic 2007 addition, the Crystal. It's one of Canada's premier museums and an essential Toronto stop.

### 2 Path for Thought

From the ROM, go west along Bloor St, then turn south (left) through the 1901 Queen Alexandra Gateway to the **Philosopher's Walk**. The path meanders through the northeast grounds of the University of Toronto's St George Campus, with beech trees and oaks providing shade.

### 3 Oxbridge Inspiration

Emerging at the south end of the Philosopher's Walk, turn right (west) toward the spires of **Trinity College** on Hoskin Ave. Erected in 1925, the building took inspiration from the hallowed Gothic halls of England's Oxford and Cambridge universities. Trinity's light-flooded chapel was designed by the renowned British architect Sir Giles Gilbert Scott.

### 4 Modernist Design

A quick detour west across Devonshire Pl reveals strikingly contrasting architecture in **Massey College**, an angular 1960s brick creation that combines Modernist lines with Gothic-inspired flourishes.

### 5 Art & Architecture

Double back along Hoskin Ave and walk 100m south on Tower Rd to **Hart House**. An early-20th-century, ivy-clad Gothic Revival building, it functions as a community space for students and staff. Also here is the university's respected Canadian-art gallery, open to all.

### 6 College on the Green

Dip south through the Soldiers' Tower, an evocative memorial to WWI and WWII, then turn right to reach **University College**. Combining British, Italian and other influences, the 1850s-building overlooks the enormous grassy expanse of King's College Circle, with views of the CN Tower in the distance.

### 7 Landmark Rotunda

Cross over to the south side of King's College Circle to admire **Convocation Hall**, where graduations are held. Notable for its domed ceiling and columned facade, the structure dates from 1907.

### 8 Coffee Calling

Weave 400m west to Spadina Crescent, taking in the dramatic Daniels Faculty, a restored Victorian seminary with Gothic-style turrets. Then drop south along Spadina Ave to College St for a well-deserved break at **Found Coffee**, an Aussie-founded spot serving flat whites and freshly baked scones.

## EXPERIENCES

### Enjoy the Views at Casa Loma
HISTORIC BUILDING

MAP: ❶ P102 **C1**

Looming over the northern Annex from atop the Davenport Escarpment, **Casa Loma** *(casaloma.ca; adult/child $40/25)* is Toronto's only castle, though it was designed as a luxurious, 98-room Edwardian mansion inspired by medieval British architecture. This cliff was once the shoreline of glacial Lake Iroquois, from which Lake Ontario derived, and fantastic city views emerge as you head up via the Baldwin Steps from Spadina Rd.

The mansion was built from 1911 to 1914 for wealthy businessman Sir Henry Pellatt, who brought electricity to Toronto (before losing his fortune in land speculation). With so many turrets, balconies and chandeliers, it's hard to know where to start, so download the free audio guide (around two hours; bring headphones). Highlights include a chandelier-lit library; an Italian-style conservatory; the Great Hall with its Gothic Revival style and 17th-century fireplace; and climbing the Norman Tower to an open rooftop overlooking Toronto's sprawl. A 250m-long tunnel connects the mansion with its grand stables.

### Explore the Indigenous Roots of Tkaronto
COMMUNITY CENTER, TOUR

MAP: ❷ P102 **D3**

A restored heritage building on Ishpadinaa (Spadina Rd, meaning 'highland' or 'high place' in the Ojibwe language) is the base for the 1960s-founded **Native Canadian Centre of Toronto** *(ncct.on.ca),* which celebrates the cultures of Indigenous communities that have lived in the Toronto region for thousands of years and has a range of cultural programs. Sign up ahead for a free Indigenous-led walking tour, learning about traditional ceremonies, languages and cultural practices. The on-site **Cedar Basket Gift Shop** stocks original pieces crafted by Indigenous artisans, such as beaded jewelry, delicate dreamcatchers and botanical candles.

One street east at Paul Martel Park on Madison Ave is *Interconnections,* an evocative mural by well-known Indigenous artist Joseph Sagaj, depicting myths and legends of Indigenous worldview.

### Browse Footwear at the Bata Shoe Museum
MUSEUM

MAP: ❸ P102 **E4**

If a gallery devoted to footwear sounds offbeat, you'll be pleasantly surprised by Bloor St's **Bata Shoe Museum** *(batashoemuseum.ca; adult/child $16/5).* Designed by Raymond Moriyama to resemble a stylized shoebox, the beloved museum houses 15,000 'pedi-artifacts' from around the globe, spanning 4500 years; only a small percentage is on view at any time. The semipermanent All About Shoes display in the basement charts the global history of footwear over millennia, while changing exhibitions are kept sharp, focused and stylish.

### Wander Around Old Yorkville  NEIGHBORHOOD

Yorkville's compact historical core still has the air of a small village, with its fine 19th-century buildings, interlinked squares and relatively peaceful lanes. It's a refreshing, pedestrian-friendly area to explore slowly and on foot. A great place to start is elegant Yorkville Ave, home to the 1876 **Yorkville Fire Hall** (MAP: ❹ P102 **H3**; built in yellow brick with red trim and a Yorkville coat of arms) and the beautifully porticoed 1907 **Yorkville Public Library** (MAP: ❺ P102 **H3**).

For a pause, check out the lovingly landscaped **Village of Yorkville Park** (MAP: ❻ P102 **G3**) or wander along **Hazelton Ave** to glimpse multi-million-dollar Victorian homes. In summer, **ROMWalks** (p44; *rom.on.ca*) occasionally offers excellent guided tours of Old Yorkville.

### Get into Ceramics at the Gardiner Museum  MUSEUM
MAP: ❼ P102 **F4**

A blue-and-white 18th-century Chinese moon-flask and a pair of mid-18th-century porcelain pugs from the Royal Palace in Warsaw count among the many treasures at the understated **Gardiner Museum** *(gardinermuseum.on.ca)*, which inhabits an angular limestone building opposite the ROM (p104). Three floors of entrancing exhibits travel through the history of ceramics in Europe, Asia and North America. It's interactive too, with games for kids, special exhibits and hands-on activities. The gallery was undergoing renovations at research time, so visiting arrangements may change.

### Stroll Through Koreatown  NEIGHBORHOOD
MAP: ❽ P102 **A4**

The stretch of Bloor St W just west of the Annex, between Bathurst and Christie Sts, is the epicenter of **Koreatown**, which emerged in the 1970s when Korean immigrants

---

### REVITALIZING BLOOR

In recent years, an inspired collaboration between the Bloor Annex BIA and the City of Toronto has brought a crop of functional new outdoor spaces and vibrant murals to Bloor St W, one of the city's most popular areas to wander around. Highlights of the **Bloor Street Revitalization Project** *(bloorannex.ca)* include Howland Avenue Parkette, overlooked by street artist Nick Sweetman's gorgeous *Pollinator Sweetheart* mural, and Komi Olaf's bright mural *The Band of Storytellers* at nearby Brunswick Parkette, which celebrates the neighborhood's beloved, now-closed jazz and blues venue, Brunswick House.

began settling in the area. Hangul signs, karaoke bars and restaurants serving bibimbap and housemade kimchi mingle in this lively pocket, where simply wandering around evokes its strong heritage and modern-day identity. Ideally, time your visit to enjoy a meal somewhere like Korean Village Restaurant (p111). Bordering the west end of Koreatown, **Christie Pits Park** is a favorite local hangout with baseball diamonds, sports fields and grassy slopes to relax on.

### Discover the Spadina Museum  MUSEUM, ARCHITECTURE
MAP: **9** P102 **D1**

Atop the Baldwin Steps at the north end of Spadina Rd, the **Spadina Museum** (*nationaltrustcanada.ca*) is a gracious home with beautiful Victorian-Edwardian gardens, all built in 1866 as a country estate for financier James Austin and his family. Donated to the city in 1978, it became a museum in 1984 and was painstakingly transformed to evoke the heady 1920s and '30s. Knowledgeable guides lead visitors on highly recommended (free) 45-minute tours, or you can wander the gardens independently with a self-guided leaflet.

### See a Film at Hot Docs  CINEMA
MAP: **10** P102 **B3**

In the thick of the Bloor St bustle, the acclaimed **Hot Docs Ted Rogers Cinema** (*hotdocs.ca*) screens a wonderfully varied schedule of new releases, art-house flicks, shorts, documentaries and vintage films in an Art Deco theater with a two-tiered balcony. It's also the main hub for North America's largest documentary-film festival, Hot Docs, which has been going for three decades and shows over 100 moving documentaries from all over the world each spring. For something a little different yet classically Toronto, you can't beat it.

### Take in the Toronto Reference Library  ARCHITECTURE
MAP: **11** P102 **H3**

Among the city's landmark pieces of 20th-century architecture, the **Toronto Reference Library** (*torontopubliclibrary.ca*) emerges with its mountain-like brick shape just north of the Bloor–Yonge intersection. It was designed in the mid-'70s by Canadian architect Raymond Moriyama and revolves around a grand curving atrium, where visitors are free to read while admiring the many intricacies of the building.

### Feel the Beat at Lee's Palace  LIVE MUSIC
MAP: **12** P102 **B4**

Legendary **Lee's Palace** (*leespalace.com*) on Bloor has set the stage over the years for Dinosaur Jr, Queens of the Stone Age and the Smashing Pumpkins. Kurt Cobain started an infamous bottle-throwing incident when Nirvana played here in 1990. Look for the primary-colored mural that seems to scream out front.

## LISTINGS

# Best Places for...

💲 Budget  💲💲 Midrange  💲💲💲 Top End

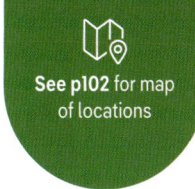

**See p102** for map of locations

## Eating

### Korean Flavors

**Korean Village Restaurant** 💲💲

 A3

One of Toronto's original Korean restaurants, now led by the second family generation. Classics include hot-stone bibimbap and *ddukbokki* (spicy rice cakes). *koreanvillageto.com; noon-9:45pm Tue-Thu, to 10:15pm Fri & Sat, to 9:30pm Sun*

**Mhel** 💲💲

 A4

Creative Korean-Japanese small plates fueled by each week's fresh hyper-local produce draw foodies to this intimate Bloor St W kitchen. *instagram.com/mhelisanchovy; 5:30-10:30pm Wed-Sun*

### Italian Dining

**Trattoria Nervosa** 💲💲

 G3

Excellent home-style pastas with southern-Italian flair (like *mafalde funghi*), on a relaxed Yorkville terrace. Great people-watching. *eatnervosa.com; 11:30am-10pm Sun-Wed, to 11pm Thu-Sat*

**Eataly** 💲💲

 H4

Pick from a fresh-pasta bar, a smart trattoria or a craft-beer counter with Italian small plates at Bloor-Yonge's stylish branch of the beloved Eataly empire. Or grab snacks from the deli. *eataly.ca; hours vary*

**Buca** 💲💲💲

 H3

Gorgeously designed Yorkville restaurant specializing in elevated, artisanal Italian cooking rooted in seasonal ingredients, including homemade pasta and charcuterie boards. *buca.ca; 5-10pm Tue-Sat*

**Piano Piano** 💲💲

 D5

The pink-walled Harbord flagship of a beloved Toronto restaurant is all about classic Italian flavors – burrata with roasted grapes, pasta carbonara. *pianopianotherestaurant.com; noon-10pm Sun-Wed, to 11pm Thu-Sat*

### Sushi & Japanese Cooking

**Sushi on Bloor** 💲

 B4

A standout among Bloor's many sushi restaurants, always packed with people devouring quality, great-value fresh rolls. *sushionbloor.com; 4-10pm Mon & Tue, noon-10pm Wed, Thu & Sun, to 10:30pm Fri & Sat*

**Aburi Hana** 💲💲💲

 G3

Chef Ryusuke Nakagawa is behind this Michelin-star marvel in Yorkville, renowned for its eight- and 12-course tasting-menu extravaganzas with Canadian flair. *aburihana.com; 6-10pm Wed & Thu, 5:30-10pm Fri & Sat*

**Fuwa Fuwa** 💲

C3

Cozy spot on Bloor serving light Japanese soufflé pancakes with sweet toppings like tiramisu or matcha. *fuwafuwapancakes.com; noon-10pm Mon-*

EXPLORE

YORKVILLE, THE ANNEX & UNIVERSITY OF TORONTO

111

Thu, 11am-10pm Fri, 10am-10pm Sat & Sun

## Yorkville Hot Spots
### Mimi Chinese 💲💲💲
 F1

The moodily lit sister to Kensington's Sunnys Chinese (p98) delivers elegant, sharing-style dishes inspired by China's diverse cuisines. The Sichuan 4ft belt noodles are a signature. *mimichinese.com; 5-11pm Tue-Thu, to midnight Fri & Sat*

### Alobar 💲💲💲
 F3

Hidden in a Yorkville court, hotshot chef Patrick Kriss' slick bar-restaurant combines expertly mixed cocktails with creative seafood-first dishes. Also has a Downtown branch. *thealobar.com; 5-10:30pm*

### Sassafraz 💲💲💲
 G3

Popular with visiting celebrities and a glamorous crowd, Sassafraz epitomizes Yorkville with its elegant yet breezy decor, sun-drenched patio and smart contemporary-Canadian menus. *sassafraz.ca; 11:30am-10pm*

### Hemingway's 💲💲
 G3

Classic Yorkville hangout, popular for its rooftop patio, after-work buzz and draft beers. Pub-like fare includes burgers, salads, zingy fajitas. *hemingways.to; 11am-2am Mon-Fri, from 10am Sat & Sun*

## Harbord Village
### Harbord Bakery 💲
 C5

Traditional-style Jewish bakery and artisanal deli going strong since the 1940s, with favorites like braided challah and fresh bagels. *harbordbakery.ca; 7am-6pm Tue-Fri, to 5pm Sat*

### Maven 💲💲
 C5

Stylish spot where Eastern European Jewish cuisine gets a lightly creative twist: fluffy challah buns, chicken schnitzel in plum sauce, earthy salads. *maventoronto.ca; 5-10pm Wed-Sat, to 9pm Sun*

### Emmer 💲
 B5

Freshly baked croissants, with flavors like pistachio, are king at this neighborhood cafe-bakery with a street-side patio. It also does oven-fresh sourdough. *emmertoronto.ca; 9am-4pm Wed-Sun*

### Dreyfus 💲💲💲
 C5

French-flavored small-plates bistro in a stylish red-brick space, with ingredients from small-scale Ontario and Québec farmers. *dreyfustoronto.com; 5.30-10pm Mon-Thu, to 10.30pm Fri & Sat*

## Mezze & Small Plates
### Paradise Grapevine 💲💲
 A4

Delicious small-plates menus of smooth cheeses and spicy peppers pair with natural by-the-glass wines. Enjoy on the year-round back patio where summer vines bloom. *noon-1am*

### Miznon 💲💲
 G3

Menus change daily depending on what's fresh at this Yorkville haunt. Rich filled pitas, housemade hummus and plenty of vegetarian picks. *miznon.ca; 11am-9pm Wed-Sat, to 8pm Sun-Tue*

🍷

# Drinking

## Coffee Time
### Slanted Door
 B3

Perfect for catching up with friends or getting emails done over coffee and a fresh pastry, this bright go-to spot in the Annex is part cafe, part gallery. *slanteddoor.ca; 8:30am-7:30pm Mon-Fri,*

9am-6:30pm Sat, 10am-6:30pm Sun

### Tiny's General Store
**33** A2

Stylish neighborhood cafe in a converted general store with outdoor benches and a small boutique stocking gourmet food products and local artisanal pieces. Near Christie Pits Park. *thetinygeneral.com; 8am-4:30pm Mon-Fri, from 9am Sat & Sun*

### Snakes & Lattes
**34** A3

Bloor St branch of a popular board-games hangout ($20 games admission), with a lively student scene and regular trivia nights to enjoy over local craft beers, coffees, milkshakes and shareable bites. *snakesandlattes.com; hours vary*

### Sam James Coffee Bar
**35** A5

A former bookshop on Harbord St is the home of the original Sam James, a prize-winning indie coffee roaster with several branches dotted around the city. *samjamescoffeebar.com; 7am-4pm Mon-Fri, from 8am Sat & Sun*

## Pubs, Cocktails & Views

### Oxley
**36** G3

Lovely British-style pub set in a 19th-century Yorkville row house, popular with a well-heeled crowd for its draft craft brews, fine wines and smart, seasonal food menus. *theoxley.com; hours vary*

### Madison Avenue Pub
**37** D3

Spread across three Victorian houses in the Annex, the casual Maddy pulls in a mostly student clientele with multiple patios, plenty of games, trivia nights and live music. *madisonavenuepub.com; 11am-2am*

### Writers Room Bar
**38** F3

High above Yorkville, the swish Park Hyatt's rooftop bar has an intriguing literary history, classic-rooted artisanal cocktails and sprawling skyline views from both the terrace and the cozy light-filled interior. *hyatt.com; hours vary*

# Shopping

## Pre-Loved Fashion

### Good Juice Box Vintage
**39** A4

Stylish vintage clothing collection, with everything from denim jackets and logo-stamped T-shirts to fluffy cardigans, located in Koreatown. *instagram.com/goodjuiceboxvintage; noon-7:30pm Sun-Fri, to 8pm Sat*

### Common Sort
**40** B3

This pre-loved specialist stocks trendy fashion and accessories, and also buys items directly from customers. There are several branches around Toronto. *commonsort.com; 11am-7pm Mon-Sat, to 6pm Sun*

## Books & Crafts

### Hanji Gifts
**41** A4

Sweet gift store devoted to Korean art and design where you can pick up treats like handmade hanji paper, original stationery and the owners' line of custom-designed cards. *hanjigifts.com; 11am-9pm*

### BMV
**42** C4

The biggest (and most popular) used bookstore in Toronto, with a spectacular selection of titles, including a large collection of Canadian literature. *bmvbooks.com; noon-7pm Sun-Wed, 10am-11pm Thu-Sat*

**See p124** for eating, drinking and shopping listings

# Explore
# Trinity Bellwoods & the West End

Stretching west from Bathurst St to High Park, the West End combines green spaces and walkable neighborhoods with some of Toronto's liveliest food, drink and arts scenes. Trinity Bellwoods is centered on a charming park of the same name and the surrounding stretch of Queen St W (also referred to as West Queen West). Ossington Ave is a trendy street for bar-hopping, fun dining and stylish strolling. Northwest is Little Portugal with its rainbows of murals and brick-built homes. This part of the city revolves around fabulous food, evening fun and public gardens, making it perfect for a leisurely wander and hopping between neighborhoods.

## Getting Around

 **Subway**
Line 2 has several stations along Bloor St that are handy for the West End, including High Park and Keele.

 **Streetcar**
Useful lines include 501 along Queen St, 505 along Dundas St, 506 along College St to High Park, and 504 along King St.

 **On Foot**
The West End is a highly pedestrian-friendly area and the best way to dive into it is by walking around its neighborhoods.

## THE BEST

**GREEN HAVEN**
High Park (p118)

**GALLERY**
Museum of Contemporary Art Toronto (p122)

**LOCAL WALK**
Little Portugal (p120)

**NEIGHBORHOOD PARK**
Trinity Bellwoods Park (p122)

**FOOD SCENE**
Ossington Ave (p124)

**Trinity Bellwoods Park (p122)**
SOCKAGPHOTO/SHUTTERSTOCK

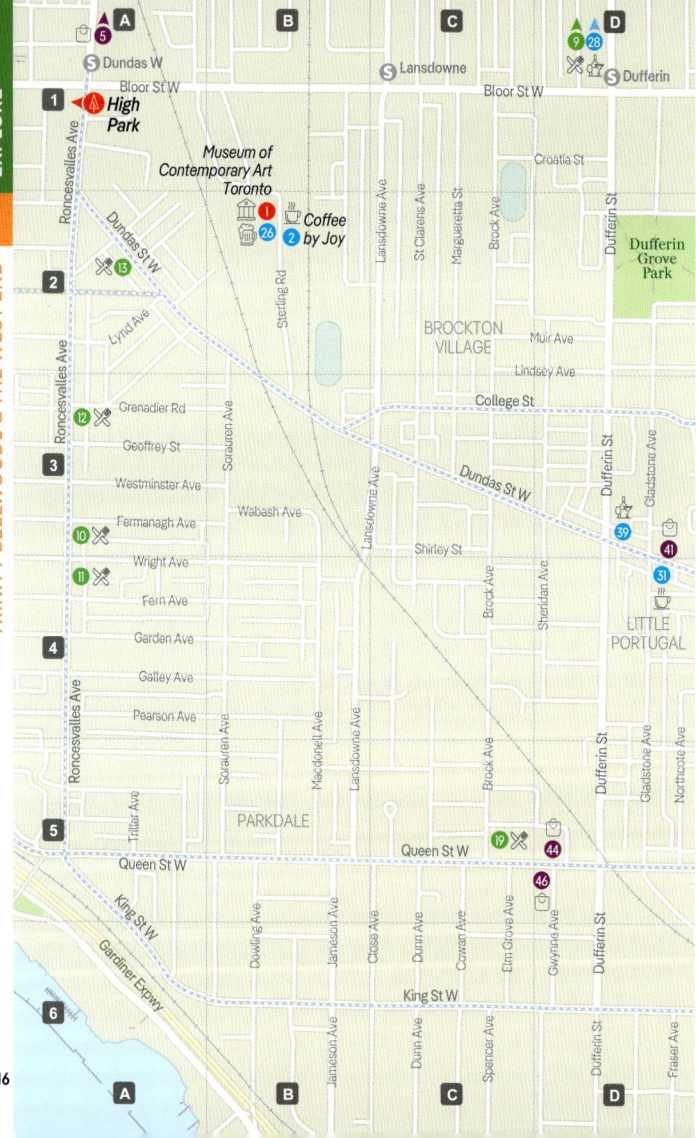

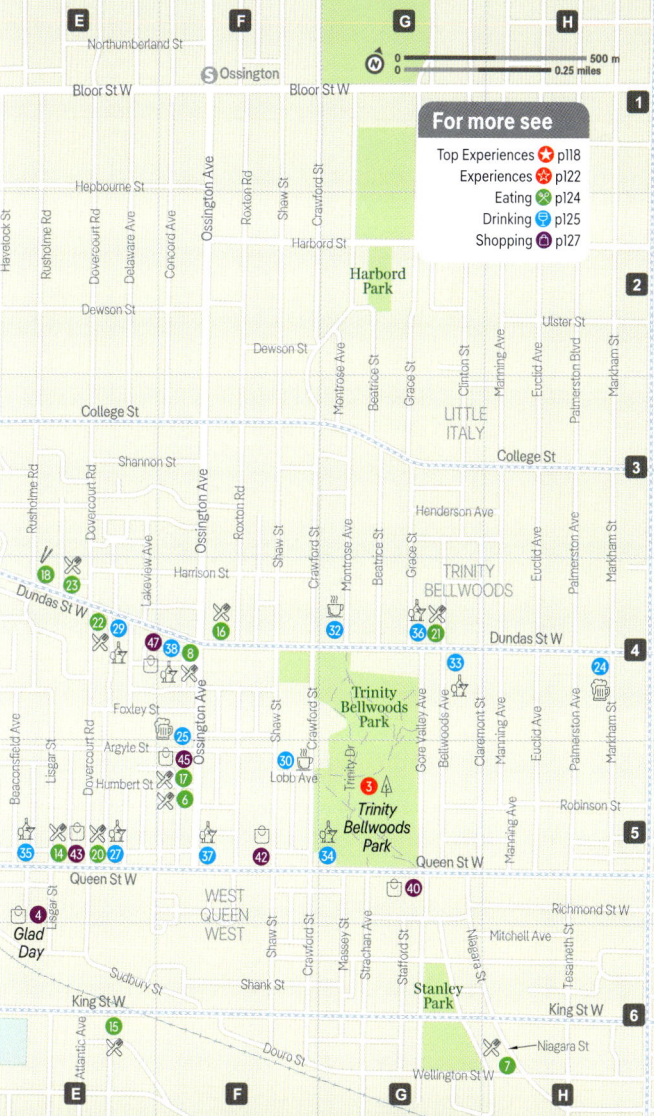

★ **TOP EXPERIENCE**

# High Park

An entrancing oasis worth traveling west for, High Park encompasses a beautiful, forested expanse with wooded trails, spring cherry blossoms, undulating hills and sparkling ponds. Torontonians come here to run, cycle, picnic and wander among the greenery, or, in summer, to catch one of the famous alfresco Shakespeare performances.

MAP P116 **A1**

**PLANNING TIP
High Park Nature Centre**, at the north end of the park, offers a rich program of guided walks, kids' events and workshops. Check schedules ahead.

Scan this QR code for more information about the park.

### Ponds & Park Highlights

A delightful time to enjoy High Park is on weekends, when all roads through it are closed to traffic. Much of the park's rolling expanses have a wild feel, lined with ponds and creeks and ideal for spotting wildlife. On the west side of the park, the **Grenadier Pond** is the largest body of water, and a great place to see waterbirds such as mallards, geese and herons. Toward the southern end is **Colborne Lodge**, a Regency-era cottage built by the painters John and Jemima Howard, who gifted the park to the city in the 1870s.

Kids are bound to enjoy meeting the llamas, peacocks and bison at the small **zoo** or hopping on the trackless **visitor train** *(adult/child $9/6)* for a ride through the greenery. During winter, an ice-skating rink opens up, while the public outdoor swimming pool is a locally popular cool-off spot in warmer months.

### Spring Blooms

If you're visiting in late April or early May, it's impossible to miss the park's cherry blossoms, which draw crowds from all over the city (and beyond). The main grove is on the west side of the

ELENA BERD/SHUTTERSTOCK

park along Grenadier Pond and up the hill toward Grenadier Cafe, with more near the Maple Leaf Flower Bed. For peak blossom-spotting, it's even possible to check how buds are progressing via the park's online 'blossom watch' service, before making the journey.

## Shakespeare in the Park

Every summer, acclaimed **Canadian Stage** (*canstage.com*) brings a fresh Shakespeare production to an open-air amphitheater in the heart of High Park. Head over early with a blanket and a picnic to soak up the atmosphere with a local crowd and enjoy the drama under the stars at one of Canada's longest-running outdoor theater events.

**QUICK BREAK**
In the heart of High Park, **Grenadier Cafe** (*grenadiercafe. net*) has low-key meals and an outdoor terrace. Or walk over to Roncesvalles Village for a bite at the diner-style Ace (p124).

## WALKING TOUR

# Walk Little Portugal

Little Portugal centers on Dundas St W between Ossington and Landsdowne Aves. Dotted with stylish restaurants and shops, it has a long history as an area where residents of Portuguese and Brazilian heritage settled from the 1950s onward. Explore stories past and present on this neighborhood itinerary.

| START | END | LENGTH |
| --- | --- | --- |
| Trinity Bellwoods Park | Dundas West Mural | 2km; 1hr |

## 1 Leafy Oasis

From Queen St W, walk through the restored early-1900s gates welcoming you into lovely **Trinity Bellwoods Park** (p122). From 1852 to 1925, this spot was home to Trinity College (originally called the University of Trinity). Skirt around the dog park bowl – where there are usually neighborhood canines running around – as you head north across the park. Maple trees dot the park's northwest corner (beautiful in fall).

## 2 Little Portugal

Turn left (west) on Dundas St for 100m to reach the moving **Amália Rodrigues mural**, painted in 2020 by Montréal artist Matthew Cadoch in honor of the great Portuguese singer credited with bringing fado to the world. Continue on to the junction of Dundas St and Ossington Ave, where a floor sign marks the border of Little Portugal.

## 3 Portuguese Crafts

The art of Portuguese crafts is celebrated in creative contemporary style at **Saudade**, a bright little boutique filled with colorfully painted pottery, regional cookbooks, crystal glassware, cabbage-leaf tableware, original jewelry and other temptations. Everything on show is made in Portugal. As you continue on, note the typical architecture of the area, with brick houses fronted by gardens hugging the street.

## 4 Custard Tarts

The next stop is just a few steps further west along Dundas St. Established in the 1960s (and now with various branches around Toronto), **Caldense Bakery** still makes traditional oven-fresh *pastéis de nata,* the traditional Portuguese custard tart said to have been born in 19th-century Lisbon.

## 5 Take a Break

Walk another 400m west along Dundas St and, if you like, stop for an espresso or a martini at all-day cafe-bar **Milou**, which has French-style menus and a warm-weather patio to relax on.

## 6 Dundas West

Wander around 500m west and you'll pass the *Three Sisters* mural depicting three Indigenous women with crops of maize, squash and beans, by Chilean Mapuche artists Paula Tikay and Aner Urra. Wrap up with José Ortega's butterfly-stamped **Dundas West mural**, at the intersection of Dundas and Sheridan Sts, a key piece of the Dundas West Open Air Museum.

## EXPERIENCES

### Be Immersed in the MOCA
GALLERY

MAP: **1** P116 **B2**

A soaring 1920 former industrial building that once produced aluminum parts has been creatively transformed into the Junction Triangle's fabulous **Museum of Contemporary Art Toronto** *(moca.ca; adult/child $14/free; Wed-Sun)*. Exhibitions by Canadian and international artists change several times each year, but are always thought-provoking and focused on contemporary themes, often including specially commissioned pieces that strikingly interact with the historical setting. It's a great place to discover Torontonian artists, too, so a visit is well worth it even if current exhibitions don't include familiar names.

For a break, the lobby houses a branch of Italian deli Forno Cultura (p125), or hop across Sterling Rd to artisanal-feel **Coffee by Joy** (MAP: **2** P116 **B2**), a cafe serving brews in handcrafted mugs.

### Hang Out in Trinity Bellwoods Park
PARK

MAP: **3** P116 **G5**

Whether on a blossom-filled spring day or when the leaves turn a thousand shades of red in the fall, **Trinity Bellwoods Park** *(toronto.ca)* is one of the city's prettiest and most-loved green spaces. The 14.6-hectare park owes its name to the 1852-founded University of Trinity (later Trinity College), which once stood here. With tennis and volleyball courts, ball diamonds and a kids' playground, it's always a hive of activity. Over 60 species of tree dot the grounds, including Sakura cherry trees that burst into baby-pink bloom, as well as ancient elms, oaks and maples. Wander through the restored iron gates overlooking Queen St at the park's south end (all that now remains of Trinity), spot the CN Tower's spire in the distance and relax on the benches for a delicious slice of Toronto life.

### Pop into Glad Day
BOOKSTORE

MAP: **4** P116 **E5**

Founded in the 1970s by influential activist Jearld Moldenhauer, **Glad Day** *(gladdaybookshop.com)* is the world's longest-running LGBTIQ+ bookstore and a beloved community landmark. Now a switched-on gathering space devoted to celebrating creativity, inclusivity and free speech, it has played an important role in defying censorship of LGBTIQ+ publications. After many years in the Village, at the time of writing it was in the midst of relocating to West Queen West (check for updates).

### Explore Roncesvalles
NEIGHBORHOOD

On the east side of High Park, **Roncesvalles Village** *(roncesvallesvillage.ca)* is an easygoing, underrated corner of Toronto that rewards those who make the detour (streetcars 501, 504, 505 or 506). The area developed mostly from the 1900s onward, attracting in particular a large Polish community. These days the main stretch is Roncesvalles Ave, a pedestrian- and cyclist-friendly space with flower-fringed sidewalks, independent shops and neighborhood restaurants. At Roncesvalles and Garden Aves, you can't miss *The Original People Leading to the Eighth Fire*, a distinctive mural by local artists Jim Bravo and Philip Cote to share the important Indigenous heritage of the Roncey area, which was once part of a trading route connecting with Lake Ontario.

A great way to get a taste of the district's spirit is on an expert-guided, small-group food walk with **Culinary Adventure Co** (p44; *adult/child $129/124*).

### Step into the Junction  NEIGHBORHOOD

Today's **Junction** *(torontojunction.ca)* – the stretch of Dundas St W between Keele St and Runnymede Rd – was founded as an independent village in the 1880s, on lands where Indigenous trading routes had previously operated for thousands of years. It became an important railway hub (hence the name) and manufacturing community and still retains many of the original factories and warehouses.

In recent years the neighborhood has grown into one of the city's most vibrant, known for its lively restaurant, bar and live-music scenes. Tempting local shops include mural-walled Type Books (p127) and the **Arts Market** (MAP:  P116 A1), an artists' collective. It's a 20-minute walk north from the Keele subway station (near High Park) and is also served by buses.

Around 2km east of the Junction, just north of the Dupont and Dufferin Sts intersection, **Geary Ave** is a former industrial district where old warehouses have been converted into shops, restaurants and breweries (p124).

---

### 🟠 SEASONAL MARKETS

During warmer months, public spaces all over Toronto spring to life with an array of open-air pop-up markets, often combining fresh produce, artisanal crafts, live music and streetfood stalls. Weekly farmers markets set up in Trinity Bellwoods Park (122), the East End's Riverdale Park (p135), the Underpass Park near Corktown Common (p69) and several other locations from around May to October. Other hits include Trinity Bellwoods' **Toronto Flower Market** *(torontoflowermarket.ca)* and the **Toronto Flea** *(torontoflea.com)* in Leslieville. Winter sees the arrival of festive markets around the city, including the outrageously popular Winter Village in the Distillery District (p63).

## LISTINGS

# Best Places for...

**$** Budget  **$$** Midrange  **$$$** Top End

See p116 for map of locations

## Eating

### Seasonal Menus

#### Union $$
**6** F5

Perfect at any time, this bistro-style Ossington address has French flair and a year-round patio. Delicious weekend brunches. *union.ca; 11:30am-10pm Mon-Fri, 10am-3pm & 5-10pm Sat & Sun*

#### Edulis $$$
**7** H6

Reservations are essential for this small, raved-about restaurant hidden off King St. Elevated menus with a Spanish influence. *edulisrestaurant.com; 6:30-11:30pm Thu, 6-11pm Fri & Sat, noon-4pm Sun*

### Middle Eastern Cooking

#### Haifa Room $$
**8** F4

Relaxed all-day corner spot on Ossington that serves a mean falafel platter, *sabich* (eggplant and salad) sandwiches and fragrantly fresh mint tea. *thehaifaroom.com; hours vary*

#### Parallel $$
**9** D1

Venture up to Geary Ave for delectable hummus, falafel, pitas, herby salads and other sharing-style bites, in the warehouse interior or on a street-side patio. *parallelbrothers.com; hours vary*

### Roncesvalles Meals

#### Ace $$
**10** A3

Creatively restyled 1950s diner. Its dinners and popular weekend brunches are bursting with fresh Canadian produce. *theacetoronto.com; 6-11pm Mon-Sat, 10am-3pm Sat & Sun*

#### Cafe Polonez $$
**11** A4

Roncey staple serving authentically tasty borscht, cabbage rolls, stuffed pierogies and other Polish classics. *cafepolonez.ca; 11am-10pm*

#### Arbequina $$$
**12** A3

Beautifully creative Palestinian-Jordanian dishes by chef Moeen Abuzaid, plus alcohol-free cocktails, in a stylish and homey space. *arbequinato.com; 5-9pm Wed, Thu & Sun, to 10pm Fri & Sat*

#### Bandit Brewery $$
**13** A2

Fun local brewer with a warehouse-like interior and a glass-fronted patio, perfect for fresh salads, burgers and fries with craft ales. *banditbrewery.ca; hours vary*

### In the Junction

#### Cool Hand of a Girl $$
see **5** A1

Cozy, vegan-friendly Mexican kitchen serving corn tacos, fresh guac and breakfasts (try the huevos rancheros) with seasonal ingredients. *coolhandofagirl.com; 8am-4pm Sun, Tue & Wed, to 8pm Thu-Sat*

#### When the Pig Came Home $
see **5** A1

This deli specializes in smoked-meat sandwiches and Jamaican patties, reflecting its owners' culinary heritages. *whenthepigcamehome.ca; hours vary*

### Noctua Bakery $
see  A1

A beautiful neighborhood bakery with a handful of tables for devouring sinfully good morning buns, twice-baked croissants and organic breads. *noctuabakery.com; 8am-5pm*

## Baked Treats & Brunch

### Forno Cultura $$
**14** E5

Design-forward space with strong espresso and delectable Italian-style bites. *fornocultura.com; 7:30am-7pm Mon-Fri, from 8am Sat & Sun*

### Mildred's Temple Kitchen $$
**15** E6

Brunch place beloved of a stylish crowd, best known for its buttermilk pancakes. *mildreds.ca; 10am-3pm Mon-Fri, from 9am Sat & Sun*

### Lakeview Diner $$
**16** F4

This 1932 Trinity Bellwoods classic has made several Hollywood appearances and serves brunch and diner fare in a picture-perfect setting. *thelakeviewrestaurant.ca; 24hr*

### Bar Koukla $$
**17** F5

Fun weekend-brunch spot on Ossington with a Greek twist. *mamakas.ca; 5:30pm-midnight Mon-Fri, from 11am Sat & Sun*

## Asian Cuisines

### Oddseoul $$
see  F5

Dive-bar vibes and terrific Korean-American comfort food, ideal for sharing, at a long-running fave on Ossington. *instagram.com/90oddseoul; 6pm-1am*

### Imanishi $$
**18** E4

Dundas West go-to for imaginative renditions of Tokyo-style dishes, like panko-crusted prawns and smooth daily sashimi. *imanishi.ca; 5:30-11pm Mon-Sat*

### BB's $$
**19** C5

It's all about creative Filipino cooking at this Parkdale hit, serving weekend brunch and delicious adobo fried chicken. *bbs.restaurant; hours vary*

### Jamil's Chaat House $$
 E5

Casual restaurant and bar specializing in inventive Pakistani snacks with plenty of spice. The tangy dahi puri is a signature. *jamils.ca; 5-11pm Wed-Sun*

## Italian Restaurants

### Bar Vendetta $$
**21** G4

Stylish Dundas St kitchen loved for its home-fresh pastas and marble-bar dining. *barvendetta.com; 5-10:30pm*

### Stefano's Diner $$
**22** E4

Plant-forward Italian with an upscale deli-meets-bistro vibe. Top bites include the eggplant-parmigiana sandwich with mozzarella. *stefanosdiner.com; hours vary*

### Enoteca Sociale $$$
**23** E4

Beautifully prepared, Roman-inspired dishes in an artfully styled interior or on the romantic European-style terrace. *sociale.ca; 5-10pm Sun-Wed, to 11pm Thu-Sat*

# Drinking

## Breweries

### Collective Arts
 H4

The buzzing Toronto taproom of a much-loved Hamilton-born brewery, with mural-covered walls, a fun terrace and its creative craft beers and cocktails on tap. *collectiveartscreativity.com; 11am-11pm*

### Bellwoods Brewery
 F4

Always busy with a local crowd, urban-chic Bellwoods pours award-winning beers to go with sophisticated small plates like Canadian-cheese boards. *bellwoodsbrewery.com; 5pm-midnight Mon & Tue, from noon Wed, Thu & Sun, noon-1am Fri & Sat*

### Henderson Brewing Company
 B2

A laid-back warehouse brewery in the Junction Triangle neighborhood with a tasting room, picnic tables and huge fermentation tanks. *shophendersonbrewing.com; 10am-10pm Sun-Thu, to 11pm Fri & Sat*

## Wine Bars

### Bar Piquette
 E5

Pick from natural wines chalked up on the board and enjoy them on the sweet back patio at this Queen St delight of a wine bar. *barpiquette.com; 5pm-late Mon-Fri, 1pm-late Sat & Sun*

### Paradise Grapevine
 D1

Popular Paradise makes some of its Niagara-grown drops on-site at its Geary Ave winery, which also has a tempting bar and a seasonal patio. There's a Bloor St branch too. *paradisegrapevine.com; 5pm-midnight Sun & Tue-Thu, to 2am Fri & Sat*

### Grape Witches
 E4

Natural-wine boutique and casual bar with a back terrace on Dundas West where you can taste by the glass. Also at Waterworks Food Hall (p45). *grapewitches.com; noon-10pm Sun-Wed, to 11pm Thu-Sat*

## Coffee Scene

### Found Coffee
 F5

Come for the lovely sunny terrace just steps from Trinity Bellwoods Park, stay for the velvety flat whites and brunchy Aussie-style bites. *found.coffee; 8am-5pm*

### Larry's Back Pocket
 D4

Little Portugal vintage-feel cafe with window seats, tempting baked goods, friendly baristas and own-roasted beans. *larrysworld.ca, 7am-5pm Mon-Fri, 8am-4pm Sat & Sun*

### Morning Parade Coffee Bar
 G4

Arty interiors and bustling atmosphere just across from Trinity Bellwoods Park. *morningparade.ca; 7am-6pm Mon-Fri, from 8am Sat & Sun*

## Cocktail Spots

### Northern Belle
 G4

Cozy up at the long bar or out on the Dundas West patio over expertly mixed classic cocktails and more creative concoctions. *instagram.com/northernbelleto; hours vary*

### Mother Cocktail Bar
 G5

Moodily styled, prize-winning cocktail bar serving ambitious mixes and made-to-order numbers. *motherdrinks.co; 6pm-midnight Mon & Sun, to 1am Tue & Wed, to 2am Thu-Sat*

### Drake Hotel
 E5

Boutique hotel, live-music venue, club and pub all rolled into one, with different areas to enjoy including the sunny rooftop bar. *thedrake.ca; hours vary*

### Rhum Corner
 G4

Fun, tropical-inspired liquid mixes with fruity

flavors in a Haitian bar that also does snacky food. *rhumcorner.com; 6pm-midnight Tue-Thu, to 1am Fri & Sat*

### All About the Vibes
**Sweaty Betty's**
**37** F5

An Ossington original, this tiny, red-lit, lounge-like bar is all about classic cocktails, a heated back patio, an inclusive space and having a good time. *sweatybettysbar.com; 3pm-2am Mon-Fri, from 1pm Sat & Sun*

**Communist's Daughter**
**38** F4

Drinks here feel like stepping back in time. Finding it is half the fun, yet the place is still packed on weekends when live music takes over. *instagram.com/thecommunistsdaughtertoronto; hours vary*

**Cry Baby Gallery**
**39** D3

Step through an art gallery in Little Portugal to discover its cool speakeasy, where original cocktails are mixed using homemade ingredients. *crybabygallery.ca; 6pm-2am Mon-Sat, from 8pm Sun*

# Shopping

### Food, Books & Crafts
**Type Books**
**40** G5

Superb independent bookstore with a lively calendar of author talks, book launches and other events. Also in the Junction. *typebooks.ca; 10am-6pm Sun-Wed, to 7pm Thu-Sat*

**Kitten & the Bear**
**41** D3

The scent of freshly baked scones wafts through the door at this cute bakery-and-store on Dundas St W. *kittenandthebear.com; 10am-5pm Tue-Sun*

**Hanji Gifts**
**42** F5

A little slice of Korea in Trinity Bellwoods. Original cards, authentic hanji paper and sweet trinkets. Also on Bloor (p113). *hanjigifts.com; 11am-7pm*

**Craft Ontario Shop**
**43** E5

A long-time promoter of local artisans, stocking ceramics, jewelry, prints and more, including pieces by Indigenous artists. *craftontario.com; 11am-6:30pm Tue-Sat, noon-5pm Sun*

### Fashion & Vintage
**Public Butter Vintage**
**44** D5

One of the city's most popular vintage stores, in Parkdale. Shelves overflow with denim jackets, floaty dresses, band T-shirts, Levi's jeans and the like. *instagram.com/publicbutter; 11am-7pm Mon-Sat, to 6pm Sun*

**Province of Canada**
**45** F5

Laid-back yet impeccably stylish clothing (sweaters, hats, T-shirts) made in Canada is the thing at this local designer. *provinceofcanada.com; 10am-6pm*

**House of Vintage**
**46** D5

Fulfil your one-of-a-kind dreams at this perfectly curated vintage boutique in Parkdale, known as one of Toronto's hottest spots for men's and women's pieces. *instagram.com/houseofvintagetoronto; noon-7pm Mon-Fri, 11am-7pm Sat, noon-6pm Sun*

**Penny Arcade**
**47** E4

Chic little vintage store in Little Portugal filled with denim shorts, pre-loved jeans, designer dresses and a few homewares. *pennyarcadevintage.com; noon-6pm*

# Explore
# East Toronto

Many East Toronto residents rank their pocket of town as the loveliest, and it's easy to see why. This part of the city is a place to enjoy some greenery without leaving the urban sprawl proper. Largely residential, it's a rewarding spot to spend time, with walkable neighborhoods, expansive parks and Evergreen Brick Works, an impressive heritage-meets-sustainability project. There's a trendy edge around Queen St E (home to breweries and boutiques), while sandy beaches and bird-rich Tommy Thompson Park await along the lakefront. Eastern enclaves like Greektown, East Chinatown and Little India show off the East End's diverse cultural background.

## Getting Around

### Walking & Cycling
East Toronto's neighborhoods are ideal for exploring on foot, with quiet residential streets and buzzing main thoroughfares. Bike paths weave along waterfront areas, particularly convenient for Tommy Thompson Park and The Beaches.

### Streetcar
The 501, 503 and 504B streetcars all run along Queen St E; the latter turns north at Broadview Ave, eventually linking up with Broadview subway station.

### Subway
Line 2 runs along Danforth Ave; useful stops include Castle Frank, Broadview, Chester, Pape, Donlands and Coxwell.

## THE BEST

**REGENERATIVE PROJECT**
Evergreen Brick Works (p132)

**CITY VIEWS**
Riverdale Park East (p135)

**GREEN SPACE**
Tommy Thompson Park (p136)

**NIGHTLIFE**
Broadview Hotel (p141)

**FAMILY FUN**
Riverdale Farm (p136)

Tree swallow, Tommy Thompson Park (p136)
PUFFIN'S PICTURES/SHUTTERSTOCK

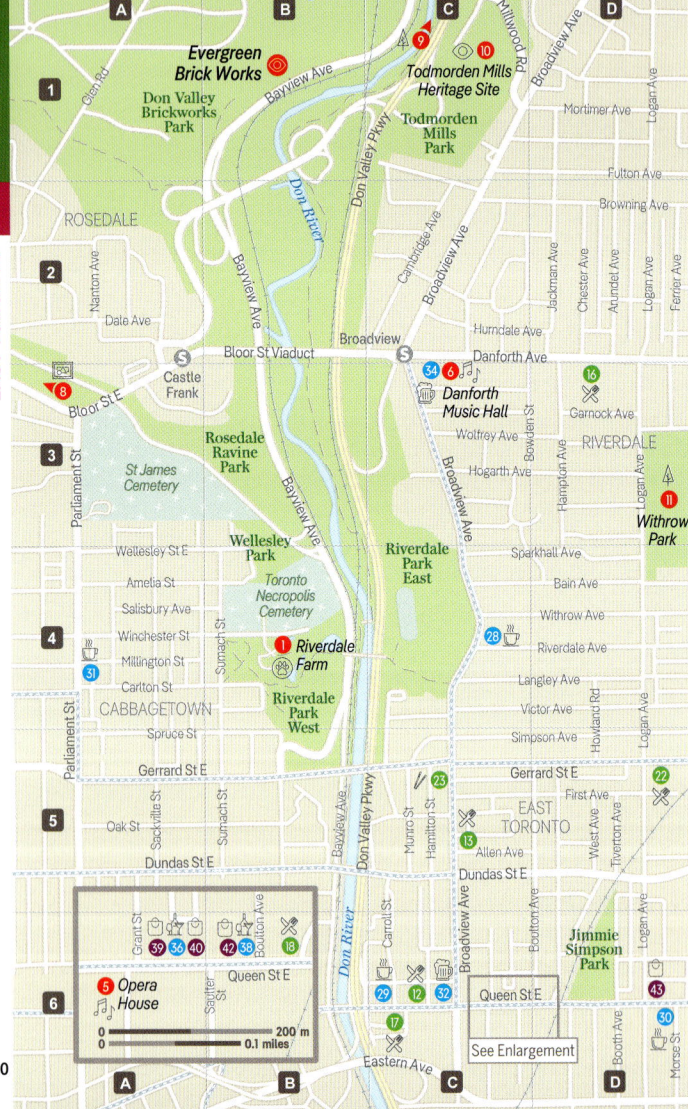

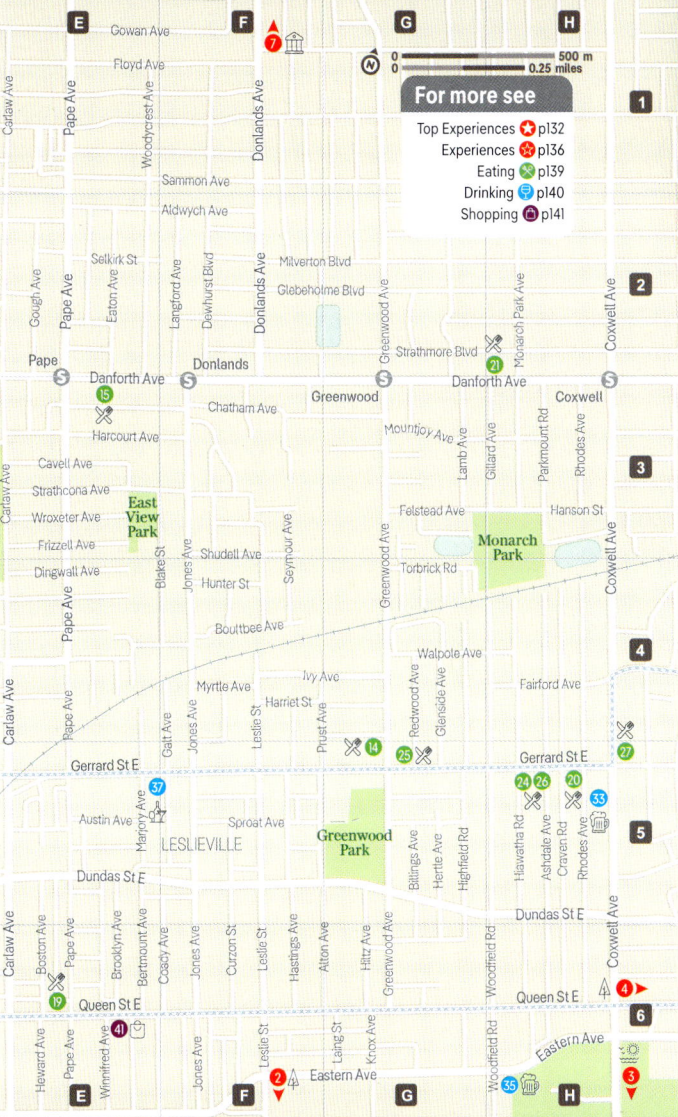

★ **TOP EXPERIENCE**

# Evergreen Brick Works

Set in a revitalized 1880s brick factory, Evergreen Brick Works is a forward-looking, LEED-certified complex and community gathering place with green wilds right on the doorstep. Various heritage buildings here are now used to engage the city's residents year-round, with art installations, a kids' garden, a farmers market and a whirlwind of events.

MAP P130 **B1**

**PLANNING TIP**
Visit with an activity in mind, such as the farmers market, a nature-trail hike or a cycling route. Excellent free one-hour tours run on Saturdays at 11am and 1pm.

Scan for opening times, transportation tips, tour details and more.

### History & Art

Founded in the late 19th century by William Taylor, the Toronto Brick Company fueled the city's construction industry for a century with its distinctive red bricks. After being abandoned in the 1980s, it was painstakingly restored by nonprofit Evergreen and reopened in 2010, with 16 heritage buildings to explore. In the former kilns building you can see where bricks were once fired, and some sections feature vibrant graffiti from parties held during its empty years.

Intriguing artworks are woven into the fabric of the complex. Don't miss Ferruccio Sardella's *Watershed Consciousness,* showing Toronto's ravine and river system in steel, copper, brass and plants; Quinn Hopkins' *Stellar Narratives: An Urban Indigenous Odyssey,* which uses technology to share Anishinaabe stories; and the reproduction of Rita Letendre's 1971 *Sunrise* by Tannis Nielsen.

### Markets & Children's Garden

The year-round **Saturday Farmers Market** is a much-loved East End event. It's a feast of fresh Ontario-grown produce (most sourced from within 200km) and sizzling street-food stalls. On Sundays

ROY HARRIS/SHUTTERSTOCK

from May to October, a fun artisanal and vintage market takes over. In winter, come for the ice-skating rink, firepits and festive markets. For kids, the **Children's Garden** is a highlight, with outdoor play areas, organized activities and gardens where little ones can get stuck into growing vegetables.

## Nature Trails

It's hard to imagine that the 16.5-hectare **Don Valley Brick Works Park** *(toronto.ca)* was once the factory's clay and shale quarry. Trails and boardwalks now weave through the forested park, passing creeks, ponds, wildflower meadows and Carolinian trees. The east-side slopes have terrific Toronto skyline views, particularly tempting in fall colors. The park links to the Beltline Trail (p136) on its west side.

**QUICK BREAK**
Part of the fun is sampling delicious bites from Brick Works' weekly markets. Alternatively, the all-day **Picnic Café** does coffees, blueberry scones and snacks like grilled-cheese sandwiches.

# Architecture & Green Spaces

This eastbound walk unites outstanding Victorian architecture, neighborhood parks and exquisite city views. Cabbagetown is believed to be North America's largest continuous expanse of preserved Victorian housing, and gives way to refreshing green spaces on the banks of the Don River.

| START | END | LENGTH |
|---|---|---|
| Cabbagetown | Queen St E | 3km; 1hr |

## 1 Neighborhood History

Begin at Carlton and Parliament Sts, easily reached on streetcar 506. Walk north along Parliament, then turn right (east) on to Winchester St, in the heart of **Cabbagetown**. The neighborhood is said to owe its name to the vegetables planted by Irish immigrants from the 1840s onward. Admire the jumble of Gothic Revival, Bay & Gable and Second Empire homes.

## 2 Historic Cemetery

After following Winchester St eastward for 500m (perhaps also peeking down Metcalf and Sackville Sts for more Victorian architecture), the **Toronto Necropolis** looms into view ahead. Dating from the 1850s, it's a rolling public space where several high-profile Torontonians have been laid to rest. Wander in through the entryway on Winchester St, a beautiful example of High Victorian Gothic architecture.

## 3 Green Corner

On the south side of the necropolis, **Riverdale Park West** dates to the late 19th century and makes a lovely spot for a break under the trees; on Tuesday afternoons in summer there's a farmers market here. Hugging the north side of the park is 19th-century-style Riverdale Farm (p136), where you can meet the animals (for free) before cutting downhill.

## 4 Skyline Thrills

Follow the pedestrian bridge across the Don Valley Parkway to reach wide-open **Riverdale Park East** (500m on from the farm), where people gather to gawp at one of the finest skyline views in town. On warm evenings, the whole place comes alive as picnic rugs are laid out for sunset-watching. In winter, the park's slopes transform into a popular tobogganing spot.

## 5 Coffee With a View

Clamber up the grassy hillside to the top of the park and cross Broadview Ave to **Rooster Coffee House** (p140). The view feels all the more magical over a brownie and a batch brew on their streetfront terrace.

## 6 Eastern Hub

From here, a rewarding option is to wander 1km south down to **Queen St E**, where some of East Toronto's standout bars and restaurants await. Along the way you'll pass through East Chinatown, which is sprinkled with murals and has a traditional archway gate by the junction of Broadview Ave and Gerrard St. Alternatively, from Rooster head 900m north to subway-served Danforth Ave.

## EXPERIENCES

### Meet Furry Friends at Riverdale Farm          FARM
MAP: ① P130 B4

On the site of the former Riverdale Zoo, where from 1888 to 1974 prairie wolves howled at night and spooked the Cabbagetown kids, **Riverdale Farm** (*riverdalefarm toronto.ca; free*) is a rural oasis on the fringes of the neighborhood. A working farm and museum since the 1970s, it delights visitors of all ages with its resident horses, cows, goats, chickens and pigs. Each morning farmers lead insightful talks focused on different animals, and you can watch the team going about the day-to-day chores. The entire place feels worlds away from the Downtown bustle.

### Explore Tommy Thompson Park          PARK
MAP: ② P130 F6

Between the Downtown waterfront and the eastern Beaches district, **Tommy Thompson Park** (*tommythompsonpark.ca*) is a wild, traffic-free haven stretching 5km out into Lake Ontario. What was once a thin spit of land is now a wildlife-rich 'urban wilderness,' created using dredgings from Toronto's outer harbor development. It's known for its birdlife, with over 300 species spotted here, including owls, herons and egrets (as well as foxes, turtles and even coyotes).

The best way to enjoy the park is by cycling its flat trails. Bike Share Toronto has a dock near the entrance on Leslie St, from where it's a 5km one-way cycle (or walk) to the lighthouse on the park's southern tip, which has magical views of the Toronto Islands and the city skyline. Around 3km in is a floating bridge, also with beautiful Downtown panoramas.

### Relax in The Beaches          BEACH, NEIGHBORHOOD

To Torontonians, **The Beaches** (or just The Beach; *to-thebeach. com*) is an upscale yet chilled-out neighborhood hugging the eastern lakefront. Though little visited by tourists, this area centered on Queen St E is a popular escape for a local crowd, especially during warmer months, with a string of tawny strands including lovely **Kew Beach** (MAP: ③ P130 H6) and a sunny boardwalk skirting along the sand. The cross-city Martin Goodman Trail (p55) passes through here, and in summer there are beachfront operators renting kayaks, canoes and paddleboards. After a spell on the waterfront, make your way through leafy **Kew Gardens** (MAP: ④ P130 H6) to Queen St E, where a chilled local dining scene awaits.

### Go Hiking or Cycling Along the Beltline          NATURE TRAIL

Extending across northeast Toronto, the **Beltline Trail** (*toronto.ca*) provides a shady and refreshing retreat for local runners, walkers and cyclists. Head here for a taste of East Toronto's rolling green nature. The trail runs along the old tracks of the failed Toronto Belt Line Railway and is officially split into three sections – York (west), Kay Gardner (near Allen Rd) and Ravine (east). A great place to pick up the Beltline is on the western edge of Evergreen Brick Works (p132), from where you can head northwest up to Mt Pleasant Cemetery (around 2km).

### Catch a Concert  LIVE MUSIC

There's always something fun happening in the East End, where several long-established live-music venues ensure a thrilling year-round lineup. Check ahead to see what's on.

Over in Riverside, the **Opera House** (MAP: 5 P130 A6; *theoperahousetoronto.com*) ranks among the city's best small spaces for concerts, DJ nights and other musical events. Over the years, this early-1900s Edwardian vaudeville hall has welcomed the likes of Nirvana, Metallica, Green Day, The Killers, Rick Astley and Rage Against the Machine.

Or drop by the hugely popular **Danforth Music Hall** (MAP: 6 P130 C3; *thedanforth.com*), a now-restored brick-walled landmark first opened in 1919 as a movie theater (and originally a sister venue to Bloor's Lee's Palace; p110). Despite the occasional temporary closure, the venue has been a fixture of the Toronto music scene since the 1970s. This is where Rihanna famously held a surprise Toronto concert in 2012, while others who have graced the stage here range from The Police to several *RuPaul's Drag Race* queens.

### BEST GREATER TORONTO AREA HIGHLIGHTS

With time (and transportation), the Greater Toronto Area is well worth exploring.

**Aga Khan Museum** *(agakhanmuseum.org; adult/child $20/10)* North America's first museum devoted to Islamic art and also an architectural feast, in North York.
MAP: 7 P130 F1

**McMichael Canadian Art Collection** *(mcmichael.com; adult/child $20/7)* Spread across rolling grounds, this beautifully located gallery north of Downtown is known for its collections of works by respected Indigenous artists and the Group of Seven, Canada's foremost landscape painters.
MAP: 8 P130 A3

**Rouge National Urban Park** *(parks.canada.ca; free)* One of North America's largest urban parks, this 79-sq-km expanse east of the city is laced with hiking trails.
MAP: 9 P130 C1

## Uncover Industrial History at Todmorden Mills
HISTORIC SITE

MAP: 10 P130 C1

Hidden away next to the Don River (and just a 1km walk or cycle from Evergreen Brick Works; p132), the **Todmorden Mills Heritage Site** *(toronto.ca; free)* immerses visitors in East Toronto's important industrial heritage. A collection of old millers' homes and other historical buildings from the 19th and 20th centuries dive into the complex's journey from gristmill, to brewery and distillery, to paper mill. Free one-hour tours are led by enthusiastic guides several times daily, though you can also explore independently (note that the site is closed on Monday and Tuesday).

The surrounding area has been transformed into a wildflower-filled nature park.

## Stroll Around Greektown
NEIGHBORHOOD

A quick subway hop across the Don River Valley from Downtown Toronto, Danforth Ave is home to one of North America's largest Greek communities. Stretching roughly from Broadview subway station east to Greenwood Ave, **Greektown** (aka the Danforth; *greektowntoronto.com*) has its roots in a post-WWII migratory wave to this part of Toronto in the 1950s and 1960s, though these days the area has grown into a deeply multicultural pocket of the city.

Wandering along the broad sidewalks, it's easy to spot blue-and-white street signs with names also appearing in Greek, long-established bakeries with counters of tempting spanakopita and loukoumades, and family-style restaurants serving meze platters, souvlaki-stuffed pita and other treats.

Just off Danforth Ave, pop into lush **Withrow Park** (MAP: 11 P130 D3; *toronto.ca*), which has play areas for kids, distant skyline views and, in summer, a popular Saturday farmers market.

# LISTINGS

# Best Places for...

$ Budget  $$ Midrange  $$$ Top End

## Eating

### Brunch & Breakfast

**White Lily Diner** $$
**12** C6
Retro-style haven awarded a Michelin Green Star for brunch-focused menus starring ingredients from the owners' organic farm. *whitelilydiner.ca; 9am-4pm Mon & Tue, to 10pm Wed-Sat*

**Lady Marmalade** $$
**13** C5
A loyal crowd flocks to this brunch-scene staple with design-driven interiors and decadent Moroccan-style scrambles and build-your-own eggs Benedict. *ladymarmalade.ca; 8:30am-3pm*

**Maha's** $$
**14** G5
Arrive early or join the line for easygoing Egyptian brunches like fava-based *foole* with falafel and feta. In Leslieville, too. *mahasbrunch.com; 8am-4:30pm Thu-Tue*

### Greek Cooking

**Athens** $$
**15** E3
Traditional dishes with fresh, local ingredients at a warmly welcoming Greektown address. Try spreads lathered on fluffy pita. *athensdanforth.ca; 11am-11pm Tue-Sun*

**Pantheon Restaurant** $$
**16** D3
Family-owned Danforth classic with a street-front patio. Known for its *saganaki* cheese served flaming. *pantheondanforth.ca; 11am-9pm Sun-Thu, to 10pm Fri & Sat*

### Baked Treats

**Blackbird Baking Co** $$
**17** C6
Glorious sourdough, creative sandwiches and fresh pastries at one of Toronto's most sought-after bakers. *blackbirdbakingco.com; 8am-6pm Mon-Sat, 9am-5pm Sun*

**Bonjour Brioche** $$
**18** B6
Oven-fresh croissants lure regulars to this French bakery-cafe on Queen E, which also serves bistro-style breakfasts. *bonjourbrioche.com; 8am-2pm Wed, to 3pm Thu-Sun*

### Creative Dining

**Avling** $$
**19** E6
Ultra-fresh ingredients and contemporary flavors await at this relaxed craft brewery, which has its own rooftop farm. *avling.ca; Tue-Sun, hours vary*

**Lake Inez** $$$
**20** H5
An atmospheric lounge-like feel with natural wines, original cocktails and drool-worthy small plates with an Asian edge. *lakeinezto.com; 5pm-midnight Wed-Sat*

**Wood Owl** $$
**21** H2
Cozy, wood-paneled wine bar on the Danforth, perfect for sipping unexpected labels alongside seasonal small plates like lemony *cavatelli*. *instagram.com/thewoodowlto; 5-11pm Tue-Thu, to 11:30pm Fri & Sat*

**See p130** for map of locations

EXPLORE · EAST TORONTO

### Wynona ❸❸❸
**22** D5

Weekly rotating menus rooted in Italian flavors at this understated Leslieville restaurant with warm-weather patio. *wynonatoronto.com; 5-11pm Mon-Sat*

### Asian Menus & Little India

### Oji Seichi ❸❸
**23** C5

Fragrant broths and fresh housemade noodles mean delectable ramen bowls at this mural-walled East Chinatown spot. *ojiseichi.com; noon-3pm Tue-Sun, 5-9pm Tue-Thu, 4-9pm Fri-Sun*

### Udupi Palace ❸
**24** H5

Light, fluffy *masala dosa* and other South Indian favorites at a long-running, all-vegetarian Little India restaurant. *udupipalaces.ca; 10am-10pm Sun-Thu, to 11pm Fri & Sat*

### Tea-N-Bannock ❸❸
**25** G5

Indigenous specialties such as three-sisters soups, sustainably fished salmon with bannock and bison burgers on fresh flybread buns. *teanbannock.ca; 3-8pm Thu, noon-8pm Fri & Sat*

## Tacos & Burgers

### Puerto Bravo ❸❸
**26** H5

Seafood-driven menus inspired by regional flavors from Tamaulipas are the hot ticket at this Mexican joint on Gerrard East. *instagram.com/puertobravo.to; noon-9pm Tue-Sun*

### Harry's Charbroiled ❸
**27** H5

Popular Toronto burger specialist serving perfectly sizzled patties (including a vegan version). Also has a branch at Waterworks Food Hall (p45). *harryscharbroiled.com; 11am-9pm*

# Drinking

## Coffee Classics

### Rooster Coffee House
**28** C4

Overlooking Riverdale Park, Rooster is busy due to its specialty brews, freshly baked pastries and street-side patio with city views. *roostercoffeehouse.com; 7am-7pm*

### Dark Horse Espresso Bar
**29** C6

Flagship location of this popular third-wave coffee spot, with communal tables, seasonal brews and sesame cookies. *darkhorseespresso.com; 7:30am-7pm Mon-Fri, from 8am Sat & Sun*

### Mercury Espresso
**30** D6

Enjoy morning coffee on the corner terrace at an easygoing local go-to serving beans from Canadian roasters. *instagram.com/mercuryespresso; 6:30am-6pm Mon-Fri, from 8am Sat & Sun*

### Jet Fuel
**31** A4

Arty spot in Cabbagetown, popular with a cycling crowd. Stop by for an espresso with a fresh-baked pastry. *jetfuelcoffee.com; 6am-5pm*

## Breweries & Pubs

### Eastbound Brewing Company
**32** C6

Try house craft beers or a pineapple margarita with delicious Mexican-inspired snacks at this top Riverside brewery. *eastboundbeer.com; hours vary*

### Godspeed Brewery
**33** H5

Respected warehouse-like beer hall crafting an eclectic lineup, including Czech lagers, Pearl Morissette wines and

Japanese-influenced dishes. *godspeedbrewery.com; 11am-9pm Sun-Thu, to 11pm Fri & Sat*

### Allen's
 C3

The tree-shaded seasonal patio steals the show at this cozy Irish pub on the Danforth, with 100-plus beers, Ontario wines and sophisticated local-produce meals. *allens.to; hours vary*

### Rorschach Brewing Co
 H6

Handy(ish) for The Beaches, this century-old house is now a creative brewery with ever-changing menus, reliably good eats and two patios. *rorschachbrewing.com; noon-9pm Mon & Sun, to 10pm Tue-Thu, to 11pm Fri & Sat*

## Cocktail & Wine Bars

### Broadview Hotel
see  C6

Drink in the skyline from East Toronto's best rooftop, with a chic outdoor terrace and glassed-in lounge. Inventive cocktails, light bites, DJs. *thebroadviewhotel.ca; 4-10:30pm Sun-Thu, to midnight Fri & Sat*

### Comrade
 A6

Queen East favorite for natural wines, local craft beers, expertly mixed cocktails and signature smashed burgers on a busy patio. *comradetoronto.com; 5pm-midnight Mon-Wed, to 2am Thu-Sat*

### Poor Romeo
 E5

Get a taste of the Gerrard E scene over housemade cocktails, fresh oysters and DJ sets at this neighborhood dive bar. The team also runs Pinkertons across the road. *instagram.com/poor_romeo_bar; 5pm-1am Mon-Tue, to 2am Wed-Fri, 3pm-2am Sat*

### Chez Nous
 B6

Queen East staple with a popular street-side patio and daily happy hours, specializing in Ontario wines and house-mixed cocktails. *cheznouswinebar.ca; 5pm-midnight Sun-Thu, to 2am Fri & Sat*

# Shopping

## Vintage Style

### Second Voyage
 A6

Bright collection of pre-loved fashion (from denim dungarees to leather jackets) and elegant vintage homewares. *secondvoyage.ca; hours vary*

### Good Juice Box Vintage
 A6

Printed T-shirts, denim jackets, cozy sweaters and other eye-catching garments fill this effortlessly cool vintage corner. *instagram.com/goodjuiceboxvintage; noon-6pm Mon-Fri, 11am-7pm Sat, noon-7pm Sun*

### Bettencourt Manor
 E6

Renowned interior-design boutique stocking vintage furnishings, as well as more suitcase-friendly products. *bettencourtmanor.com; 11am-5pm Wed-Sun*

## Books & Crafts

### Arts Market
42 B6

A collective of local artists sells work at this creative little shop, from handcrafted cards and jewelry to pottery and vintage finds. Also on Danforth Ave. *artsmarket.ca; 11am-6pm*

### Queen Books
43 D6

Lively independent Leslieville bookstore with a thoughtfully curated collection. Plenty of Toronto titles, plus literary events. *queenbooks.ca; 10am-6pm*

## ★ WORTH A TRIP

# Niagara Falls

An area of undeniable natural beauty rests alongside a bright-lights city with amusement-park-like energy in Niagara Falls. Unstoppable rushing waters surge over an arcing fault in the Niagara riverbed with thunderous force on both sides of the Canada–US border, and great plumes of icy mist rise hundreds of meters as the flows collide, entrancing thousands of onlookers.

MAP P144

**GETTING THERE**
**GO Transit** *(go transit.com)* and **VIA Rail** *(viarail. ca)* have several daily trains (two to 2½ hours) between Toronto's Union Station (p41) and Niagara Falls GO Station. **Flixbus** *(flixbus.ca)* and **Megabus** *(mega bus.com)* take 1½ to 2½ hours.

Scan for visitor and transportation info, and ticket purchases.

### Horseshoe Falls

The centerpiece of any visit are the powerful, deep-turquoise **Horseshoe Falls** (pictured). Named after their 670m curved shape, they have the highest flow rate of any waterfall in North America; at 65km/h, more than 2574 kiloliters of water per second crash into the roiling Maid of the Mist Pool. Some of the finest views (of all three falls) are from the garden-fringed walkway on the Niagara Gorge rim, south from Clifton Hill, especially around the **Table Rock** viewpoint. Arrive early to beat the crowds. Continue south toward the Niagara Parks Power Station (p144) for up-close views of the Niagara River rushing toward the Horseshoe Falls.

With **Journey Behind the Falls** *(niagara parks.com; adult/child $29/19)*, you'll descend 38m by elevator to exposed viewing platforms within Horseshoe Falls (poncho at the ready); the roar of the water echoes all around and the experience is available even in winter. If you're planning to see other sights too, consider buying an **Adventure Pass** *(adult/child from $69/45)*, which includes a selection of attractions plus local WEGO bus journeys. From mid-May to mid-October, a dazzling fireworks show lights up the falls and the sky above each night at 10pm.

VADIM 777/SHUTTERSTOCK

### Bridal Veil Falls & American Falls

Rushing waters between Luna and Goat Islands create the **Bridal Veil Falls** on the US side, just 17m wide. The falls form a perfect bridal-like veil that crashes onto mammoth rocks, 55m below. Next to them, the **American Falls** create an astonishing 260m-wide curtain of charging white water, where daytime rainbows often appear.

### Cruises & Other Activities

An ever-growing flurry of activities guarantees views of the falls from every angle. Nothing beats the thrill of sailing into the spray of the thundering Horseshoe Falls with **NIAGARA CITY CRUISES** (*cityexperiences.com; adult/child $42.95/27.95*). Half the fun is getting soaked by the mist – despite donning a hot-pink poncho. Or take the gentle elevator ride to the top of the 158m-tall

**QUICK BREAK**

For smart seasonal Ontario-produce menus, make reservations at **Flour Mill Scratch Kitchen** or **AG Inspired Cuisine**. Clifton Hill's **Niagara Brewing Company** does pub-style dishes and beers brewed on-site.

**GETTING AROUND**
The local WEGO bus service *(niagaraparks.com)* links Niagara Falls GO Station with attractions in the city and along the Niagara River Pkwy. Connect to the Niagara-on-the-Lake shuttle from the Floral Clock stop (green line).

**Skylon Tower** *(skylon.com; adult/child $20/9)*, a concrete spire with spectacular views, especially in the morning when the early mist clings to the falls or on a summer night with fireworks bursting into the sky. Thrill-seekers can zip-line past the American Falls or take it all in from above with a helicopter ride.

### Niagara Parks Power Station

Reopened to visitors in 2021 following a prize-winning 25-million-dollar restoration, the **Niagara Parks Power Station** *(niagaraparks.com; adult/child $32/21)* was Canada's first hydroelectric power station. As you roam through the soaring artifact-filled main hall, self-guiding audioguides and expert-led tours (with an extra charge) bring the building's history to life, from its pioneering beginnings harnessing the energy of the Horseshoe Falls in 1905 up to the eventual

2006 closure. Then hop in a glass-fronted elevator to travel 55m down into the station's eerie tunnel, which emerges at a wow-inducing viewing platform overlooking the Horseshoe Falls almost at river level.

## Walk by the Water

Escape Niagara Falls by venturing 7km north along the Niagara River Pkwy to the serene **Niagara Glen Nature Reserve** *(niagaraparks.com; free)*. Long before the falls morphed into a tourism hub, this area held important significance for Indigenous communities. Today, a staircase leads down into the tranquil Carolinian forest, connecting with nine rugged hiking trails (the main loop is 2.1km), where you'll hear little more than the rush of rapids. Or will you? Collaborating with Indigenous elders, Indigenous radio broadcaster Michele-Elise Burnett and her son William L Reich have curated an immersive, downloadable self-guided audio tour, Rekindling All Our Relations: An Indigenous Journey of the Niagara Glen. It encourages visitors to connect with the natural world through storytelling, music and elder knowledge while weaving through this special space.

Also nearby is the **White Water Walk** *(niagaraparks.com; adult/child $20/13)*, a forest-shaded boardwalk overlooking Class VI white-water rapids, and the spine-tingling 1916 **Whirlpool Aero Car** *(niagaraparks.com; adult/child $20/13)*, which still trundles across the gorge suspended 60m above the swirling water. The neighboring **Botanical Gardens** *(niagaraparks.com; free)* offer a soothing retreat among 40 hectares of greenery, including a beautiful arboretum, recovered indigenous meadows and thousands of summer roses; there's also a **butterfly conservatory** *(adult/child $20/13)* with 2000 fluttering creatures.

### NIAGARA-ON-THE-LAKE

With more time, don't miss the chance to explore Niagara-on-the-Lake, one of North America's best-preserved 19th-century towns. Just 25km north of Niagara Falls, it's a refreshingly laid-back world of rolling vineyards, superbly restored homes and offbeat breweries. Wine world aside, highlights include the late-18th-century **Fort George** *(parks.canada.ca)*, key to the War of 1812, and **Niagara-on-the-Lake Museum** *(notlmuseum.ca)*.

# Toronto Toolkit

| | |
|---|---|
| **Family Travel** | 148 |
| **Accommodations** | 149 |
| **Food, Drink & Nightlife** | 150 |
| **LGBTIQ+ Travelers** | 152 |
| **Health & Safe Travel** | 153 |
| **Responsible Travel** | 154 |
| **Accessible Travel** | 156 |
| **Nuts & Bolts** | 157 |

**Kensington Ave (p93)**
JMT PHOTOGRAPHY AND MEDIA/SHUTTERSTOCK

# Family Travel

From gorgeous green spaces to unbeatable museums, Toronto counts among Canada's most thrilling cities for families with kids. There's often an outdoors focus too, whether you're keen to go kayaking *en famille* or relax on Lake Ontario's beaches.

### Eating Out

Toronto's family-friendly attitude and immense variety of cuisines mean you'll have no trouble finding welcoming places to eat with little ones. Many kitchens stay open all day (making early meals easy) and plenty of places offer kids menus. Baby high chairs are readily available on request – even in breweries.

### Sights & Attractions

Most museums, galleries and other attractions offer discounted (or free) access for children; it's best to check age restrictions ahead. Many of them also have a big family-friendly focus, with sensory experiences for kids, creative play centers, dedicated tours and special events. Stroller access or parking/storage is readily available. Some attractions don't allow certain styles of baby carriers (check in advance).

### TRANSPORTATION

Kids aged 12 and under travel for free on all TTC services, and there are also discounted youth fares for those aged 13 to 19. Buses and streetcars have dedicated stroller space. Most subway stations have elevator access.

### Cooling Off

The beaches of the **Toronto Islands** (p58) are a family favorite for paddling in Lake Ontario. In warmer months, many parks and squares have splash pads for kids, such as **Sugar Beach** (p55).

### Playgrounds

Fun playgrounds are dotted all over Toronto. Scan this code to find one nearby.

### Baby Changing & Breastfeeding

Most sights, restaurants and malls have baby-changing facilities; some larger venues have nursing rooms. Parents have the right to breastfeed in public.

# Accommodations

Options range from friendly hostels and neighborhood B&Bs to chic boutique hotels and luxe five-stars. Book ahead.

## Where to Stay if You Love...

###  Arts & Must-See Sights
**Entertainment & Financial Districts (p33)** Downtown buzz, performing-arts theaters, waterfront access and the CN Tower. Great choice of hotels and restaurants (budget permitting), plus transportation.

**HOW MUCH FOR A NIGHT IN A...**

Hostel dorm bed
**from $45**

Midrange hotel
**from $200**

Fancy boutique or four-star-plus hotel
**from $300**

###  History & Markets
**Old Town & Distillery District (p61)** Red-brick architecture, neighborhood dining, a historical atmosphere and the city's finest market. Mostly midrange hotels. Also convenient for exploring East Toronto.

###  Art & Food Scene
**Chinatown, Kensington Market, Little Italy & Queen West (p87)** Trendy neighborhoods with street art, multicultural cuisine and great thrifting, but limited accommodations choices.

###  Museums & Shopping
**Yorkville, the Annex & University of Toronto (p101)** Luxury hotels, restaurants and boutiques in Yorkville. Midrange and budget sleeps and neighborhood feel in the Annex. Great galleries.

###  LGBTIQ+ Scene
**Downtown Core & the Village (p73)** The noisy core is central, with great transportation and wide-ranging accommodations, but some unsavory areas. Smaller B&Bs in the LGBTIQ+ hub of the Village.

**OUR PICK**

**We Love to Stay in...**

**Trinity Bellwoods & the West End (p115).** Trinity Bellwoods has exciting bars, restaurants and boutiques. Green spaces, good transportation and local vibes abound in the West End. The only catch? Accommodations are limited to a couple of boutique hotels and private rentals. Adjacent Queen West is a popular alternative.

# Food, Drink & Nightlife

### Allergies & Intolerances

In restaurants, servers will ask straight away about any allergies or intolerances that they need to be aware of. Restaurants aren't legally required to mark allergens on menus, though some choose to do so (ask if in doubt about any ingredients). Many places offer gluten-free, vegetarian or plant-based options or can adapt other dishes on request.

### TIP CREEP

Tip creep is growing among businesses where service is minimal, and is a hot topic among Torontonians. Tipping isn't compulsory, but is appreciated for good service or regular haunts.

---

### CUTTING COSTS

Toronto's food-and-drink scene is one of its big attractions, but it can also wreak havoc on your budget. Thankfully, many places offer popular happy hours for drinks or *aperitivo* hours with snacks in the mix. Lunchtime set menus are another great way to rein in expenses while still dining well.

---

### Alcohol Regulations

Ontario has expanded liquor sales, enabling thousands of (licensed) grocery stores to sell alcohol, along with LCBO (Liquor Control Board of Ontario) shops, which are still major players. As of 2025, you can legally drink alcohol in over 50 Toronto parks. Ontario's legal drinking age is 19.

### HOW TO... Pay the Bill

Once the end of a meal rolls around, you'll want to ask for the bill (not the check). Sometimes it arrives without being requested once servers have cleared the table of final dishes.

**Splitting the bill** If you've dined with other people, it's perfectly acceptable to ask to pay individually; staff will bring you an itemized bill showing what you've consumed personally (even down to split dishes).

**Tipping** A 13% HST charge is added to prices that appear on menus. Most places prioritize card payments, which will offer suggested percentages for a tip (most people in Toronto tip around 18% to 22% in restaurants these days).

## PRICE RANGES

The following prices refer to the average price of a main course.

**$** less than $18
**$$** $18 to $28
**$$$** more than $28

## OPENING HOURS

**Cafes** 7am to 6pm
**Restaurants** 11am to 3pm & 5pm to 10pm (but varies)
**Bars** Varies; often noon to midnight Sunday to Wednesday, to 2am Thursday to Saturday.

## Going Out

### Where to drink

Toronto is strong on day-to-night cafe-bars where you can just as happily sip a morning espresso as an evening margarita. Tucked-away dive bars, chic cocktail spots, rooftop bars with skyline views, laid-back wine bars and creative breweries are some of the city's other temptations. Many drinking venues have food options.

**Best areas** There's always a local scene to dive into wherever you are. The Trinity Bellwoods/Ossington/Little Portugal area is great for bar-hopping, as is College St W. East Toronto is known for its breweries. Church St in the Village has the main LGBTIQ+ scene.

**Clubs** Toronto's clubbing culture centers on the Entertainment District, where restaurants start the party and dance floors go until late. Cover charges vary, but sit in the $20 to $30 range. Most clubs open around 9pm Thursday to Sunday, but don't get busy until later.

## HOW MUCH FOR A...

**Cocktail** $14

**Poutine** $15

**Dumplings** $10

**Craft beer** $8

**Burger** $12

**Specialty coffee** $4.50

**Taco** $5

FROM LEFT: ETORRES/SHUTTERSTOCK, SERHIY SHULLYE/SHUTTERSTOCK, YUESTOCK/SHUTTERSTOCK

# LGBTIQ+ Travelers

Toronto is a highly LGBTIQ+-friendly city, and was North America's first city to legalize same-sex marriage, in 2003.

## Gayborhoods

**Church–Wellesley Village**, often referred to as the Village, has been the epicenter of Toronto's LGBTIQ+ scene since the 1980s. Many of the city's famous Pride celebrations happen here. At any time of year, its Church St strip pulls in a fun-loving crowd with welcoming pubs and restaurants, relaxed patios, cheeky drag shows and late-night clubs. Beloved haunts include **O'Grady's on Church** (p85) and **Woody's** (p80). After dark, people spill into the streets, especially on weekends.

Elsewhere, **Queen West** emerged as an arty destination for the LGBTIQ+ community in the 1970s, becoming known as Queer West. While many community venues in this area have closed down, there is still a bit of a scene a little further west, including **Sweaty Betty's** (p127) on Ossington Ave.

Other LGBTIQ+-friendly neighborhoods include Kensington Market, the Annex, Cabbagetown and Leslieville.

**OUR PICKS**

**Pride Toronto**
Timing your trip to coincide with **Pride Toronto** (pridetoronto.com) in June means joining the fun at one of the largest LGBTIQ+ festivals in the world. Events are spread across an entire month, culminating in millions of people packing into Yonge St for the hotly anticipated Pride Parade.

**GLAD DAY**
Toronto is home to the oldest surviving LGBTIQ+ bookshop on the planet. **Glad Day** (p122) is a key part of community history.

 **ON STAGE**

Check what's on at long-running LGBTIQ+ theater company **Buddies in Bad Times** (p81), in the Village.

### Resources

- **xtramagazine.com** Toronto-based digital magazine and platform for the LGBTIQ+ community.
- **the519.org** Church St community hub, offering support and programs.
- **egale.ca** National LGBTIQ+ advocacy organization, with a focus on research and education.

# Health & Safe Travel

Toronto is a safe city to visit and to live in by North American standards, but there are a few things to keep in mind.

### INSURANCE

A policy that includes both medical coverage and other travel issues is essential. Canada has an excellent healthcare system, but it is expensive to access as a visitor. Some credit cards include travel insurance, so it's worth checking before buying a separate policy.

### Keeping Safe

While in general Toronto is a safe city to wander around, there are a couple of areas where it's important to be extra aware of your surroundings and avoid walking alone, especially at night. This includes some sections of Yonge St north of College St toward Bloor, as well as some parts of Cabbagetown South. If in doubt, take an alternative route or hop in a taxi or rideshare.

### Tap Water
Tap water is clean and safe to drink. Water fountains are widely available, so bring a refillable bottle.

FROM LEFT: ZMOTIONS/SHUTTERSTOCK, TIMQUO/SHUTTERSTOCK

## QUICK INFO

### Security
Always lock bikes, or better yet bring them inside if possible.

### Fare evasion
Punishable with fines of up to $425 on TTC.

### Traffic
Take care crossing streets, as there can be some aggressive driving.

### Cannabis

Canada legalized the personal use of cannabis in 2018, and you will likely see licensed 'pot shops' alongside regular stores on many streets in Toronto. Note that it is not legal take cannabis across Canada's international border, so do not try to bring any in or take any home with you.

---

**AIR QUALITY**

In recent years, smoke from increasing wildfires in other parts of Canada has affected Toronto's air quality. Keep up to date via Canada's Air Quality Health Index *(weather.gc.ca)*.

# Responsible Travel

Follow these tips to leave a lighter footprint, support local businesses and have a positive impact on communities.

### Indigenous Experiences
Many local initiatives raise awareness about Toronto's Indigenous history, heritage and cultures. The **Native Canadian Centre of Toronto** (p108) fosters conversation, hosts regular events, sells crafts by Indigenous artisans and offers walking tours led by Indigenous guides. If you're heading to Niagara Falls, don't miss the audioguide sharing Indigenous world views for anyone visiting the beautiful **Niagara Glen** (p145).

### Walks with Purpose
Join a guided tour with **Heritage Toronto** (p69), whose team of experts organize fascinating historical and cultural walks that often showcase traditionally overlooked communities. Routes change each season.

### OUR PICK
**Evergreen Brick Works**

East Toronto's **Evergreen Brick Works** (p132) is an impressive, LEED-certified environmental center in a restored industrial-era building, with community events and a farmers market.

### Get Around by Bike
Head out on two wheels for low-impact explorations. The **Martin Goodman Trail** (p55) tracks along Toronto's waterfront, while bike lanes abound across the city. Other great places to discover by bike are **Tommy Thompson Park** (p136; also an important refuge for birds and other wildlife) and the **Toronto Islands** (p58), both traffic free.

### Resources
- **destinationtoronto.com** The city's tourist board publishes ideas for sustainably minded itineraries.
- **naturecanada.ca** This conservation charity is devoted to protecting Canada's wildlife.

MICHAEL DECHEV/SHUTTERSTOCK

## LOCAL CRAFTS

Support the work of local artisans by picking up pieces at independent, community-focused shops like **Craft Ontario** (p127) or **Arts Market** (p99). Or find pre-loved clothing at **Common Sort** (p113) or Kensington Market's vintage boutiques (p94).

### Green Meals

Toronto's culinary scene is big on fresh, Ontario-grown produce, so picking wonderful restaurants that prioritize local producers is easy. Enjoy brunch at **White Lily Diner** (p139) in Riverside, which has been awarded a Michelin Green Star for its sustainable ethos.

Neighboring brewery **Avling** (p139) is known for having its own rooftop vegetable garden, while the West End's **Union** (p124) is a favorite for farm-to-table dining. Refill shops for self-caterers are all over town too, and farmers markets are a regular event, often popping up in parks and other venues.

### DRINKING WATER

Toronto's public spaces are well equipped with drinking fountains, so there's no need to buy plastic-bottled water. **Scan this QR code to find your nearest fountain.**

### Climate Change & Travel

It's impossible to ignore the impact we have when traveling; Lonely Planet urges all travelers to engage with their travel carbon footprint, which will mainly come from air travel. While there often isn't an alternative, travelers can look to minimise the number of flights they take, opt for newer aircrafts and use cleaner ground transportation, such as trains. One proposed solution — purchasing carbon offsets — unfortunately does not cancel out the impact of individual flights. While most destinations will depend on air travel for the foreseeable future, for now, pursuing ground-based travel where possible is the best course of action.

The **UN Carbon Offset Calculator** shows how flying impacts a household's emissions

The **ICAO's carbon emissions calculator** allows visitors to analyse the $CO_2$ generated by point-to-point journeys

# Accessible Travel

### Public Transit
All TTC buses, streetcars and subway trains are accessible for wheelchair and scooter users, with allocated space. At the time of writing, 55 out of 70 subway stations had elevator access to train platforms. Several local companies offer private accessible transportation services, such as **Wheelchair Taxi Toronto** (wheelchairtaxi.online).

### Museums & Sights
The majority of Toronto's galleries, museums and other sights are accessible for wheelchair users and also offer large-print visiting materials. Some, such as the **Royal Ontario Museum** (p104), provide free wheelchairs. The **CN Tower** (p36) has even developed a wheelchair-accessible Edge Experience.

### OUR PICK
As one of Canada's leading art museums, the **Art Gallery of Ontario** (p90) continually strives to be more inclusive and accessible. The gallery is fully accessible and offers free wheelchairs and walkers for guests to use (book ahead if possible). It is also compatible with GPS-based app BlindSquare for blind visitors. Large-print materials for current exhibitions can be downloaded online.

### EXPERIENCES FOR BLIND VISITORS
**Blind Roadrunners** (blindroadrunners.ca) is an inclusive weekly running club based in Toronto, while **Blind Sailing Canada** (blindsailing.ca) organizes accessible excursions out on the water. Reach out in advance to join in.

### Accommodations
Modern hotels have elevators, wider doors, adapted rooms and other accessible services. Smaller hotels (often refurbished Victorian homes) can be less accessible. It's best to check ahead.

--- **AT THE AIRPORT** ---

Toronto's airports have strong accessible services and facilities, including providing wheelchairs for travelers to use. Anyone requiring mobility assistance should contact their airline at least 48 hours ahead.

### Resources
- **AccessNow** provides information on accessible parks, trails, hotels, restaurants and more, with a handy map.

# Nuts & Bolts

## Opening Hours
Opening hours vary throughout the year.

**Banks** 8am-5pm Monday to Friday; some open 9am-noon Saturday

**Restaurants** breakfast 7-11am, lunch 11am-3pm, dinner 5-10pm; some open all day

**Bars** noon-midnight Sunday to Wednesday, to 2am Thursday to Saturday (though varies hugely)

**Clubs** 9pm-3am Thursday to Saturday

**Shops** 10am-7pm Monday to Thursday, to 9pm Friday and Saturday, noon-5pm Sunday

**Supermarkets** 7am-10pm

## QUICK INFO

**Time zone**
Eastern Time (GMT/UTC -5; -4 during daylight savings)

**Emergency number**
911

**Population**
City of Toronto 3 million; Greater Toronto Area 7 million

## Washrooms
There are usually free public washrooms in malls and transportation hubs. Washrooms in private businesses are often locked and only available to customers.

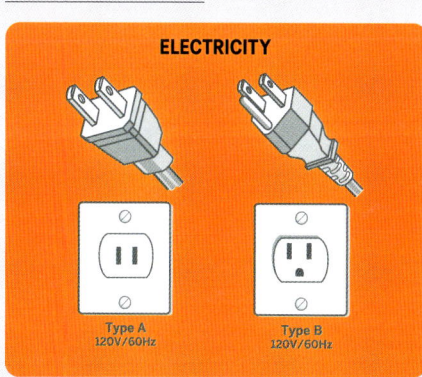

## Public Holidays
Banks, schools, government offices and many private businesses close on public holidays.

**New Year's Day** January 1

**Family Day** Third Monday in February

**Good Friday** March/April

**Victoria Day** Third Monday in May

**Canada Day** July 1

**Civic Day** First Monday in August

**Labour Day** First Monday in September

**National Day for Truth & Reconciliation** September 30 (federal statutory holiday)

**Thanksgiving** Second Monday in October

**Christmas Day** December 25

**Boxing Day** December 26

## Smoking
Smoking and vaping are banned in all restaurants, bars, sports arenas and other enclosed public spaces.

# Index

**Sights p000**  Map pages p000

*see also* separate subindexes for:
- **Eating p161**
- **Drinking p163**
- **Shopping p163**

### 401 Richmond 42

**A**

accessible travel 156
accommodations 23, 149
activities, *see individual activities*
**Adelaide Hall 42**
**Aga Khan Museum 137**
air quality 153
airports 24
**Algonquin Island 58**
**Allan Gardens Conservatory 81-2**
allergies 150
**Amália Rodrigues mural 121**
**American Falls 143**
animals 118, 136
Annex, the, *see Yorkville, the Annex & University of Toronto*
aquarium 39
architecture 7
architecture tours 40-1, 69, 134-5
arriving 24
**Art Gallery of Ontario 90-1**
artworks 8, *see also* public art

**B**

**Barbara Hall Park 79**
**Bata Shoe Museum 108**
bathrooms 157
beaches 11
 Beaches, The 136
 Hanlan's Point Beach 59
 HTO Park 53
 Kew Beach 136
 Sugar Beach Park 55
 Sunnyside Beach 53, 56
 Ward's Island Beach 58
**Beaches, The 136**
**Beltline Trail 136-7**
**Berczy Park 67, 68**
bicycle travel, *see cycling*
birds 58, 69, 136

Bloor Street Revitalization Project 109
boat travel 24, 26, 56, 58, 143
books 29
**Botanical Gardens 145**
**Bridal Veil Falls 143**
**Buddies in Bad Times Theatre 81**
bus travel 24, 25, 27
business hours 157

**C**

**Cabbagetown 135**
**Cameron House 96**
**Camões Square 96**
Canadian National Exhibition 23
**Canadian Stage 69, 119**
cannabis 153
canoeing 54
car travel 26
**Casa Loma 108**
**Cat on a Chair 93**
**Cathedral Church of St James 67**
**Centre Island 58**
children, travel with 15, 148
Chinatown, Kensington Market, Queen West & Little Italy 87-99, **88-9**
 drinking 99
 experiences 94-6
 food 97-9
 itineraries 92-3, **92**
 shopping 99
 top experience 90-1
 transportation 87
 walking tours 92-3, 95, **92**
**Christie Pits Park 110**
**Church of the Holy Trinity 81**
Church-Wellesley Village, *see Village, the*
churches 41, 67, 81
cinemas 29, 43, 110
**City Hall 44, 80**

climate 22, 155
clubs 80, 126, 151, 152 *see also* entertainment, live music
**CN Tower 36-7**
**Corktown Common 69**
**Coronation Park 53**
costs 1, 27, 148, 150, 151
cruises 56, 143
cycling 26, 154
 Beltline Trail 136-7
 Martin Goodman Trail 49, 55
 Old Toronto 68
 Toronto Islands 58
cycling tours 44
 Old Toronto 68
 Waterfront 52-3, **52**

**D**

**Danforth Music Hall 137**
**David Pecaut Square 41**
disabilities, travelers with 156
**Distillery District 63, 67**, *see also Old Town & Distillery District*
Distillery Winter Village 23, 63
Doors Open Toronto 22, 80
Downtown Core & the Village 73-85, **74-5**
 drinking 85
 experiences 80-3
 food 84-5
 itineraries 78-9, **78**
 shopping 85
 top experience 76
 transportation 73
 walking tours 78-9, 83, **78**
drinking & nightlife 13, 150-1, *see also individual neighborhoods,* Drinking *subindex,* entertainment
drinking water 155
driving 26
**Dundas West mural 121**

## E

East Toronto 129-41, **130-1**
  drinking 140-1
  experiences 136-8
  food 139-40
  itineraries 134-5, **134**
  shopping 141
  top experience 132-3
  transportation 129
  walking tours 134-5, **134**
**Eaton Centre 82**
**Ed Mirvish Theatre 83**
**El Mocambo 96**
electricity 157
**Elgin & Winter Garden Theatre 76**
emergency number 157
entertainment 12, see also cinemas, live music, performing arts, sports, theaters
Entertainment & Financial Districts 33-47, **34-5**
  drinking 46-7
  experiences 42-4
  food 45-6
  itineraries 40-1, **40**
  shopping 47
  top experiences 36-9
  transportation 33
  walking tours 40-1, 44, **40**
events, see festivals & events
**Evergreen Brick Works 132-3**
**Exhibition Place 53**

## F

**Fairmont Royal York 41**
family travel 15, 148
farms 136
ferries 24, 26, 58
festivals & events 22-3
  Canadian National Exhibition 23, 53
  Distillery Winter Village 23, 63
  Doors Open Toronto 22, 80
  Luminato Festival 23
  Na-Me-Res Pow Wow & Indigenous Arts Festival 51
  National Indigenous Peoples Day 22
  Pride Toronto 22, 81
  Rhubarb! 81
  Taste of Little Italy 96
  Toronto Fringe Festival 23
  Toronto International Film Festival 22, 43
films 29
Financial District, see Entertainment & Financial Districts
**Flatiron Building 67**
food 6, 150-1, see also individual neighborhoods, Eating subindex, vegetarian travelers
food tours 44, 94, 123
**Fort George 145**
**Fort York 51**
**Four Seasons Centre for the Performing Arts 42**
free activities 15

## G

gardens, see parks & gardens
**Gardiner Museum 109**
**Gateway 93**
gay travelers, see LGBTIQ+ travelers
**Gibraltar Point Lighthouse 58**
**Graffiti Alley 95**
**Greektown 138**

## H

**Hanlan's Point Beach 59**
**Harbourfront Centre 53, 54**
health 153
**High Park 56, 118-19**
hiking 136, 137, 145, see also walking, walking tours
history 7
  Distillery District 63
  Fort York National Historic Site 51
history tours 68, 69
**Hockey Hall of Fame 38, 41**
**Horseshoe Falls 142**
**Horseshoe Tavern 96**
**Hot Docs Ted Rogers Cinema 110**
**HTO Park 53**
**Humber Bay Arch Bridge 53**
**Huron Square 93**

## I

indigenous experiences 10, 108, 154
insurance 153
itineraries 16-19

## J

Jack Layton Ferry Terminal 58
**Junction 123**

## K

kayaking 54
**Kensington Market 92-3, 94-5**, see also Chinatown, Kensington Market, Queen West & Little Italy
**Kensington Market Garden Car 93**
**Kew Beach 136**
**Kew Gardens 136**
**Koreatown 109-10**

## L

**Lee's Palace 110**
LGBTIQ+ travelers 152
  Buddies in Bad Times Theatre 81
  Crews & Tangos 80
  Glad Day 122
  O'Grady's On Church 85
  Out on the Street 80
  Pride Toronto 81
  Woody's 80
Little Italy 95-6, see also Chinatown, Kensington Market, Queen West & Little Italy
**Little Italy mural 96**
**Little Norway Park 53**
**Little Portugal 120-1, 120**
live music
  Adelaide Hall 42
  Cameron House 96
  C'est What 71
  Danforth Music Hall 137
  Ed Mirvish Theatre 83
  El Mocambo 96
  Horseshoe Tavern 96
  Lee's Palace 110
  Massey Hall 82
  Opera House 137
  Reservoir Lounge 69
  Rex 96
  Roy Thomson Hall 42
Luminato Festival 23

## M

**Maple Leaf Gardens** 79
markets 63, 64-5, 92-3, 94, 123, 132-3
**Martin Goodman Trail** 55
**Massey Hall** 82
**McMichael Canadian Art Collection** 137
money 21
motorcycle travel 26
**Museum of Contemporary Art Toronto** 122
museums 8
music, *see live music*

## N

**Nathan Phillips Square** 79, 80
National Indigenous Peoples Day 22
**Native Canadian Centre of Toronto** 108
neighborhood experiences 14
**Niagara Falls** 142-5, **144**
**Niagara Glen Nature Reserve** 145
**Niagara Parks Power Station** 144
**Niagara-on-the-Lake** 145
**Niagara-on-the-Lake Museum** 145
nightlife, *see drinking & nightlife*

## O

**Old City Hall** 79
Old Town & Distillery District 61-71, **62**
drinking 70-1
experiences 68-9
food 70
itineraries 66-7, **66**
shopping 71
top experiences 63-5
transportation 61
walking tours 66-7, 68, 69, **66**
**Old Yorkville** 109
opening hours 157
**Opera House** 137
**Osgoode Hall** 79

## P

parks & gardens 11
*Pasture, The* 41
**PATH** 43-4
performing arts

Four Seasons Centre for the Performing Arts 42
Harbourfront Centre 54
Young Centre for the Performing Arts 69
**Philosopher's Walk** 107
planning
booking 20
clothes 20
etiquette 20
money 21
tips 20
Toronto basics 20-1
population 157
**Post Office** 68
**Power Plant Contemporary Art Gallery** 54
Pride Toronto 22, 81
public art 132
Amália Rodrigues mural 121
Bloor Street Revitalization Project 109
*Cat on a Chair* 93
*Dreaming* 41
*Dreamwork of the Whales* 53
Dundas West mural 121
*Flight Stop* 82
*Gateway* 93
Graffiti Alley 95
Little Italy mural 96
*Mountain* sculpture 41
*Pasture, The* 41
street art 28
StreetARToronto 95
public holidays 157
public toilets 157
public transportation 27

## Q

Queen West 93, *see also* Chinatown, Kensington Market, Queen West & Little Italy

## R

**Reservoir Lounge** 69
responsible travel 154-5
**Rex** 96
rideshare 24, 26
**Ripley's Aquarium of Canada** 39
**Riverdale Farm** 135, 136
**Riverdale Park East** 135
**Riverdale Park West** 135

**Rogers Centre** 42
**Roncesvalles Village** 122
**Rouge National Urban Park** 137
**Roy Thomson Hall** 42
**Royal Alexandra Theatre** 42
**Royal Ontario Museum** 104-5, 107

## S

safe travel 153
**Sankofa Square** 79, 82
**Scotiabank Arena** 44
**Sharp Centre for Design** 95
shopping, *see individual neighborhoods,* Shopping *subindex*
**Skylon Tower** 144
smoking 157
**Spadina Museum** 110
**Spadina Quay Wetlands** 55
sports
Christie Pits Park 110
Hockey Hall of Fame 38
Maple Leaf Gardens 79
Rogers Centre 42
Scotiabank Arena 44
**St Andrew's Presbyterian Church** 41
**St Lawrence Hall** 67
**St Lawrence Market** 64-5, 67
stand-up paddleboarding 54, 59
**Steam Whistle Brewing** 43
street art, *see public art*
**StreetARToronto** 28, 95
streetcar travel 25
**Sugar Beach Park** 55
**Sunnyside Bathing Pavilion** 56
**Sunnyside Beach** 53, 54, 56
**Sunnyside Gus Ryder Outdoor Pool** 56
sustainability 155
swimming 28, 56

## T

**Table Rock** 142
tap water 153
taxis 24, 26
**TD Gallery of Indigenous Art** 41
**Textile Museum of Canada** 83
theaters
Buddies in Bad Times Theatre 81
Canadian Stage 69, 119
Ed Mirvish Theatre 83

Elgin & Winter Garden Theatre 76
Royal Alexandra Theatre 42
Young Centre for the Performing Arts 69
**TIFF Lightbox** 43
time zone 21, 157
tipping 21, 150
**Todmorden Mills Heritage Site** 138
toilets 157
**Tommy Thompson Park** 136
**Toronto Dominion Bank Building** 79
Toronto Fringe Festival 23
Toronto International Film Festival 22, 43
**Toronto Islands** 58-9
**Toronto Music Garden** 53, 55
**Toronto Necropolis** 135
**Toronto Railway Museum** 43
**Toronto Reference Library** 110
train travel 24, 25, 27
tram travel 25
transportation 24, 25-7
travel seasons 22
traveling with kids 15, 148
**Trinity Bellwoods Park** 121, 122
Trinity Bellwoods & the West End 115-27, 116-17
drinking 125-7
experiences 122-3
food 124-5
itineraries 120-1, 120
shopping 127
top experience 118-19
transportation 115
walking tours 120-1, 120

**U**

**Union Station** 24, 41
University of Toronto 106-7, 106
see also Yorkville, the Annex & University of Toronto

**V**

vegetarian travelers
Avelo 84
Cà Phê Rang 97
Cool Hand of a Girl 124
Impact Kitchen 57
Kinton Ramen 70
Miznon 112

Pai 45
Udupi Palace 140
**Village of Yorkville Park** 109
**Village, the 80, 152,** see also Downtown Core & the Village

**W**

walking 28, 43-4, 55, 68, 69, 107, 109, 133, 136, 145, 154
walking tours 44
Chinatown & Kensington Market 92-3, 92
Downtown Core & the Village 78-9, 83, 78
East Toronto 134-5, 134
Entertainment & Financial Districts 40-1, 40
Little Portugal 120-1, 120
Old Town & Distillery District 66-7, 68, 69, 66
Queen West 95
University of Toronto 106-7, 106
Yorkville 109
**Ward's Island** 58
**Ward's Island Beach** 58
washrooms 157
Waterfront 49-57, 50
cycling tours 52-3, 52
drinking 57
experiences 54-6
food 57
itineraries 52-3, 52
top experience 51
transportation 49
weather 22
West End, see Trinity Bellwoods & the West End
Whirlpool Aero Car 145
White Water Walk 145
white-water rafting 145
**Withrow Park** 138

**Y**

**Yorkville Fire Hall** 109
**Yorkville Public Library** 109
Yorkville, the Annex & University of Toronto 101-13, 102-3
drinking 112-13
experiences 108-10
food 111-12
itineraries 106-7, 106

shopping 113
top experience 104-5
transportation 101
walking tours 106-7, 109, 106
**Young Centre for the Performing Arts** 69

**Z**

zoo 118

# Eating

7 West Cafe 84
360 Restaurant 37

Aburi Hana 111
Ace 124
Afuri Ramen 84
AG Inspired Cuisine 143
Alder 46
Alo 98
Alobar (Entertainment District) 46
Alobar (Yorkville) 112
Amsterdam Brewhouse 57
Arbequina 124
Athens 139
Avelo 84
Avling 139

Bandit Brewery 124
Bar Goa 70
Bar Isabel 97
Bar Koukla 125
Bar Raval 97
Bar Vendetta 125
Baro 46
BB's 125
Beso by Patria 46
Blackbird Baking Co 139
Bonjour Brioche 139
Boxcar Social 57
Buca 111

Cà Phê Rang 97
Cafe Belém 99
Café Diplomatico 96
Cafe Polonez 124
Caldense Bakery 121
Campechano 45

Carousel Bakery 65
Chefs Hall 45
Chef's House 70
Cherry St Bar-B-Que 57
Conejo Negro 98
Cool Hand of a Girl 124
Cubano Kings 45

DaiLo 98
Dipped Donuts 93
Don Alfonso 1890 57
Dreyfus 112
Druxy's ROM Café 105

### E

Eataly 111
Edulis 124
El Rey Mezcal 98
Emmer 112
Enoteca Sociale 125

### F

Fika 99
Flour Mill Scratch Kitchen 143
Forno Cultura (King West) 46
Forno Cultura (Queen St W) 125
Fuwa Fuwa 111

Golden Diner Family
    Restaurant 85
Good Behaviour 99
Grenadier Cafe 119
Grey Gardens 98
Gus Tacos 97
Gusto 101 46
Gusto 501 70

Haifa Room 124
Harbord Bakery 112
Harry's Charbroiled 140
Hemingway's 112
House of Gourmet 97

### I

Imanishi 125
Impact Kitchen 57

Jamil's Chaat House 125

Khao San Road 45
Kinton Ramen 70
Korean Village Restaurant 111

### L

La Carnita 45
Lady Marmalade 139
Lake Inez 139
Lakeview Diner 125
Lao Lao Bar 84
Lee 46

### M

Maha's 139
Maven 112
Mhel 111
Miku Toronto 57
Mildred's Temple Kitchen 125
Mimi Chinese 112
Miss Likklemore's 46
Miznon 112
Mother's Dumplings 98

### N

Nabulu Coffee 84
Nami 70
Nguyen Huong 97
Niagara Brewing Company 143
Noctua Bakery 125
North of Brooklyn 85

Oddseoul 125
Oji Seichi 140
Okonomi House 84

Pai 45
Pantheon Restaurant 139
Paradise Grapevine 112
Parallel 124
Patrician Grill 70
Piano Piano 111
Puerto Bravo 140

Queens Quay Terminal 57
Quetzal 98

Rasta Pasta 98
Restaurant 20 Victoria 70
Richmond Station 45
Riviera 59
Rol San 97
Rooster Coffee House 84

### S

Salad King 84
Sassafraz 112
Senator Restaurant 85
Seven Lives 98
Simona 57
Smoke's Poutinerie 45
Som Tum Jinda 84
St Lawrence Market 64-5
St Urbain Bagel 65
Stackt Market 46
Stefano's Diner 125
Sud Forno 46
Sunnys Chinese 98
Sushi on Bloor 111
Swatow 97

### T

Tea-N-Bannock 140
Terroni 70
Trattoria Nervosa 111

### U

Udupi Palace 140
Union 124

### V

VUE Bistros 37

### W

Waterworks Food Hall 45
When the Pig Came Home 124
White Lily Diner 139
Wonton Hut 97
Wood Owl 139
Works 70
Wynona 140

Yummy Yummy Dumplings 98

# Drinking

Allen's 141
Amsterdam Brewhouse 57
Arvo Coffee 71
Bar Piquette 126
Bar Pompette 96
Bar Raval 97
Bar Volo 85
BarChef 96
Bellwoods Brewery 126
Birreria Volo 99
Boxcar Social 57
Broadview Hotel 141
Buvette Pacey 71
C'est What 71
Chefs Hall 45
Chez Nous 141
Collective Arts 125-6
Communist's Daughter 127
Comrade 141
Crews & Tangos 80
Cry Baby Gallery 127
Dark Horse Espresso (Chinatown) 99
Dark Horse Espresso (East Toronto) 140
Dark Horse Espresso (Spadina Ave) 42
Dark Horse Espresso (Waterfront) 57
Dineen Coffee Company 46
Drake Hotel 126
Eastbound Brewing Company 140
Evangeline 47
Fahrenheit Coffee (Old Town) 67
Fahrenheit Coffee (Richmond St W) 47
Found Coffee (College St) 107
Found Coffee (Trinity Bellwoods) 126
Godspeed Brewery 140
Grape Witches 126
Hair of the Dog 85
Hale Coffee 47
Harriet's Rooftop 47
Henderson Brewing Company 126
Jet Fuel 140
Jimmy's Coffee 47
King Taps 47
Larry's Back Pocket 126
Library Bar 47
Library, The 91
Lisbon Hotel 71
Made Rite Coffee 99
Madison Avenue Pub 113
Melrose on Adelaide 47
Mercury Espresso (Corktown) 71
Mercury Espresso (East Toronto) 140
Mill Street Brewery 71
Milou 121
Morning Parade Coffee Bar 126
Mother Cocktail Bar 126
Nabulu Coffee 84
Niagara Brewing Company 143
Northern Belle 126
O'Grady's On Church 85
Oxley 113
Pamenar 99
Paradise Grapevine 126
Petty Cash 47
Picnic Café 133
Poor Romeo 141
Reservoir Lounge 69
Rhum Corner 126
Rooster Coffee House (Jarvis St) 84
Rooster Coffee House (King E) 71
Rooster Coffee House (Riverdale Park) 135, 140
Rorschach Brewing Co 141
Runaway Cafe 59
Sam James Coffee Bar 113
Slanted Door 112
Snakes & Lattes 113
Sneaky Dee's 99
Steam Whistle Brewing 43
Sweaty Betty's 127
Tiny's General Store 113
Triple A Bar 71
Waterworks Food Hall 45
Woody's 80
Writers Room Bar 113

# Shopping

Arts Market (Dundas St W) 123
Arts Market (East Toronto) 141
Arts Market (Little Italy) 99
Ben McNally 85
Bettencourt Manor 141
Blackbird Vintage Finds 71
BMV 113
Boho Chachkies 95
Bungalow 95
Cedar Basket Gift Shop 108
Common Sort 113
Courage My Love 94
Craft Ontario Shop 127
Dead Dog Records 85
Eaton Centre 82
Flying Books 99
Geary Ave 123
Glad Day 122
Good Juice Box Vintage (East Toronto) 141
Good Juice Box Vintage (Koreatown) 113
Hanji Gifts (Koreatown) 113
Hanji Gifts (Trinity Bellwoods) 127
Hi Kensington 95
Hoi Bo 71
House of Vintage 127
Kensington Ave 93
Kensington Market 94
Kitten & the Bear 127
Out on the Street 80
Peace Collective 71
Penny Arcade 127
Province of Canada 127
Public Butter Vintage 127
Queen Books 141
Saudade 121
Second Voyage 141
Sonic Boom 99
Spacing Store 42, 47
St Lawrence Market 64-5
Toronto Flea 123
Toronto Flower Market 123
Type Books 127
Well 47
Wildlife Thrift Store 71

# Send Us Your Feedback

We love to hear from travelers – your comments help make our books better. We read every word, and we guarantee that your feedback goes straight to the authors. Visit lonelyplanet.com/contact to submit your updates and suggestions.

Note: We may edit, reproduce and incorporate your comments in Lonely Planet products such as guidebooks, websites and digital products, so let us know if you are happy to have your name acknowledged. For a copy of our privacy policy visit lonelyplanet.com/legal.

### Acknowledgements

Cover photograph: Flatiron Building (or Gooderham Building; p67). Diego Grandi/Shutterstock

Back photograph: View of downtown Toronto from CN Tower (p36) observation deck. Erman Gunes/Shutterstock

## THIS BOOK

The 3rd edition of Lonely Planet's Toronto guidebook was researched and written by Isabella Noble. This guidebook was produced by the following:

**Destination Editor**
Caroline Trefler

**Coordinating Editor**
Kellie Langdon

**Cartographer**
Julie Sheridan

**Production Editor**
Kellie Langdon

**Image Researcher**
Gwen Cotter

**Assisting Editors**
Holly Alexander, Liana Cafolla, Clifton Wilkinson

**Cover Researcher**
Giada de Agostinis

**Thanks to**
Fergal Condon, Darren O'Connell, Charlotte Orr, Katelyn Perry, Pia Peterson, Saralinda Turner

Although the author and Lonely Planet have taken all reasonable care in preparing this book, we make no warranty about the accuracy or completeness of its content and, to the maximum extent permitted, disclaim all liability arising from its use.

All rights reserved. No part of this publication may be copied, stored in a retrieval system, or transmitted in any form by any means, electronic, mechanical, recording or otherwise, except brief extracts for the purpose of review, and no part of this publication may be sold or hired, without the written permission of the publisher. Lonely Planet and the Lonely Planet logo are trademarks of Lonely Planet and are registered in the US Patent and Trademark Office and in other countries. Lonely Planet does not allow its name or logo to be appropriated by commercial establishments, such as retailers, restaurants or hotels. Please let us know of any misuses: lonelyplanet.com/legal/intellectual-property.

Paper in this book is certified against the Forest Stewardship Council™ standards. FSC™ promotes environmentally responsible, socially beneficial and economically viable management of the world's forests.

Published by Lonely Planet Global Limited
CRN 554153
3rd edition – May 2026
ISBN 978 1 83758 422 2
© Lonely Planet 2026
10 9 8 7 6 5 4 3 2 1
Printed in China